They're Gone! Now What?

A Grief Journey from Self-Torment to Soul Transformation

Mavis Rowe

Copyright © 2022 Mavis Rowe

All rights reserved. No part of this book may be reproduced, distributed or transmitted in any form by any means, graphic, electronic, or mechanical, including photocopy, recording, taping, or by any information storage or retrieval system, without the permission in writing from the publisher, except in the case of reprints in the context of reviews, quotes, or reference.

Unless otherwise indicated, scripture quotations are from the Holy Bible, New Revised Standard Version. All rights reserved.

For more information: m.rowe.lcsw@gmail.com

ISBN: 978-0-578-35317-3

Dedication

This book is dedicated to my moms: Annette Gaskins and Lucy Rowe and to all the angels who have transitions since I began the journey of recording these thoughts. I will love and miss you always.

Acknowledgements

First, I'd like to thank my children (or Jewels): Renita, Rowmon, Quiamony, Kesiara, Armecia, and Nai'lah. Seeing you prosper gives me the strength to keep moving even when I want to give up. You are truly my greatest blessings. I love you.

Finally, I'd like to thank my rock, my husband, Malcolm. I feel eternally blessed that God saw fit for our paths to intertwine. Malcolm, you are the answer to every prayer I never knew I needed to pray. Your strength, wisdom, and endless encouragement bolsters my confidence and makes me feel I can do anything. I love you babe to the core of my soul.

Contents

Foreword 1
Introduction: Driving Blind 4
Chapter 1: The End.. 8
Chapter 2: The Months After............................. 20
Chapter 3: Beaten Down 32
Chapter 4: Memory Lapse 38
Chapter 5: Compounded Loss 46
Chapter 6: Conflicting Faith.............................. 53
Chapter 7: Cracks In The Clouds 65
Chapter 8: Action Steps 73
Chapter 9: Finding Focus................................... 85
Chapter 10: New Anchors.................................. 95
Chapter 11: Now What? 106
About The Author...116

Foreword

Grief refuses to be ignored. It called me to the floor, inviting me to dance as if to comfort me; however, the song ended in the middle of the dance. I've never forgotten the music, venue or the occasion for this particular dance. How could I? Grief is an overwhelming experience that's impossible to forget, and equally as difficult to explain. I can't tell you how often I've struggled to remember even minor details as I went through it. Eventually, finding the fortitude to process my grief morphed into rewriting the music and polishing the details.

...a beautifully orchestrated mess.

They're Gone, Now What?, is an exploration in navigating grief (*both ours and others'*) to foster a keen awareness that death is more than an ending, it paves the way to miraculous – albeit sometimes turbulent, beginnings. Reading this book has forced me to revisit the most devastating memories of dealing with my own loss. It's been personal, and painful. See, my first run-in with grief was when my father died at a young age. I was loaded with emotions, but few words. I never properly grieved, if there's a *proper* way to do it. I didn't know it then but failing to address how my father's death affected me would resurface in a major way when I suffered loss again.

If there's anything I've learned about loss is, it has the ability to offend. This book serves as a reminder that it's hard, but we can deal with it. It's possible to manage grief and find the value in the *loss*, no matter how long it's been. Ignoring grief diminishes our capacity to feel; indulging it expands our ability to grow from it.

In this work, Mavis Rowe reminds us that there is life after loss. I wish I could promise that this account of deep love and grave loss, could somehow abdicate us from our responsibility of navigating our own grief. I can't. If I did, it would simply be untrue. However, I can ask you to consider that living through grief is a common experience for all of us. Candidly writing about it on the other hand, isn't. In fact, most of us avoid thoughts of grief and rarely develop the courage to examine the events or archive them in a book. Mavis Rowe transparently does both.

This book grants permission to live our mistakes, create a map from our missteps, and recognize our strength as we become more of who we have the potential to be. Loss is one of those things that reminds us of what we cannot control. In this book, Mavis Rowe boldly invites us to recognize the opportunities that living, loving, and losing people, creates. Read and indulge this book, with the full awareness that you are not alone.

Here, Mavis has created a way to help navigate personal experiences of loss and love. Her account is brave in its ability to uncover common wounds and allow us to identify perceived failure while providing processes that aid in personal recovery. This book is the gift that I didn't know I needed. Encountering it has encouraged me to be brave, again. It has encouraged me to be curious, again. But most of all, it has encouraged me to recognize my losses as opportunities to live fully, and to dance with intention one more time; to dance with the plan of remembering the venue, the occasion and all the beautiful and painful details.

By: Alva Kershaw, LCSW, MDIV

INTRODUCTION

Driving Blind

The *fourth* dream was the charm for me. Prior to writing this book, I had five dreams about God's protection and control over my life for two months. Dream number four was the biggest revelation: I turned my mother into an idol – a god. In the dream, I was traveling on the highway. Traffic was normal as I plodded along without a worry. Other cars were on the road as well, moving at their own pace. Like me, no one else seemed to be in a rush. At one point I'd gotten so comfortable, even though I was driving, I took my eyes off the road and reclined my chair, not focused on the highway, or anything else.

Girl, you better pay attention and make sure you're not about to swerve into another lane, I thought after traveling that way for a while. Curious but not panicked, I straightened up and refocused. I was safe in my lane, driving along at the same steady, relaxed pace as other cars passing by. Nothing seemed amiss, so I continued on to my destination.

The next morning, I woke up, momentarily forgetting about the dream. Later as I drove to work, I asked God for answers. I wanted – no I needed, to know where I was going and the itinerary once I got there. As soon as I asked, the Lord immediately reminded me of this dream. See, in the dream, my destination, the mechanics of driving, how fast I traveled, and the outcome weren't my concerns. Although I was in the driver's seat, my only responsibility was trusting God to control the wheel, set the pace He wanted me to travel, and get me to the destination in a safe, timely manner. All I had to do was be willing to let Him navigate everything around me, knowing I was safely in the Creator's care.

Traveling to work that day, I traveled the same speed as I had in the dream, blown away by the level of freedom and peace coming over me as I zipped down the road. Suddenly, everything fell into place within my spirit. I was being launched into my destiny. That dream helped me finally surrender to God, allowing Him to take His rightful place in my life. For so many years, I worried about everyone and everything around me. So, when I asked God to clear up my confusion, He reminded me of my relationship with my mother.

My idol.

For the first 18 years of my life, my mother was my ALL. She protected, guided, chastised, and comforted me during the most significant time of my life, which laid the foundation for the woman I am today. As long as Mom was there, I felt safe. Having her there was the security I needed to know I'd be fine. So, God taking the person who mattered most in my life away, shattered me almost beyond repair. I clamored to rewind time and bring her back, but retracting time is impossible. Death can't be recalled. What hurt the most was believing I didn't need anything or anyone else but Mom. When her life ended, mine did, too.

…until it began again.

Between these pages, I'm using my experience with death to free others from the shackles of grief. It is my hope that you - the reader, will develop a clear understanding that everything happening in our lives – even death, impacts our destiny. Therefore, we must value and respect every situation, good or bad. It's important to trust the process, even when we can't understand what God is doing. Like taking our loved ones away.

This book is about disruption, and how I managed to survive significant losses while adapting to the changes the Holy One orchestrated as He created new life for me. It's about how to move into purpose and let go of the painful past to embrace a bright future. Within these pages, let my life serve as an example of how dying to self and living in divine destiny can propel us into boundless blessings. All we have to do is learn how to place our cares in the hands of our Creator.

Life doesn't end after death. There is more to come; however, it won't manifest without releasing the one we lost, and anchoring ourselves to the Almighty. It's His strength that propels us into destiny, not our own. Don't be afraid to let your loved one rest in peace, or allow yourself to live abundantly under God's grace, protection, and loving care.

It's time to set both your loved one and yourself free. It's possible to be comfortable without knowing where the road is going. Trust that Jehovah is leading us into greatness. As long as we have that trust, our holy GPS will guide us to our destination on time to fully walk in purpose. It is my hope that reading this book will give you the power to stop being tormented by unresolved grief and live freely in the presence of God.

CHAPTER 1

The End

My mother's death was the best thing that ever happened to me.

I was an inquisitive child. Always asking how things work, why things are the way they are, and about my family origins. Like after watching the mini-series *Roots,* I asked Mom if our family lifted newborns before the vast African sky as Kunta Kinte's family had done the night of his birth. It wasn't the same; however, I was super excited when she told me the tradition in our family when a child was born was to have the oldest male family member walk the perimeter of the family home, sharing our family's rich history. Somehow, this tradition bypassed me, but I wasn't bothered. At least I had a story to pass along to my future children, so our history would not be lost.

There was another time when Mom was busy in the kitchen, and I asked her about the circumstances surrounding my birth, which had been on my mind for quite a while. Because in order to relay history, we have to start with knowing what that history is, right? You should know Mom birthed seven other children (I'm seven years younger than my closest sibling). I wanted to know why she had me, why didn't I know who my father was, and why she wanted to keep me, since he wasn't around.

"Why am I here?" I asked.

"Because I needed a daughter to raise on my own without the interference of other people," she casually replied as she went on about her business.

My mind raced to my oldest sister, Linda, who was born when Mom was 16. Mom was learning to be a mother when her own mother suddenly died; the grief was too much, so she moved to Virginia to live with her grandparents who eventually raise my sister. In Virginia, she had two sons before she finally got married and had four more children: twin sons and two daughters. What happened next is a bit convoluted. I don't have a complete grasp on the details because there are so many missing pieces. Somehow, my sisters ended up being raised by their paternal grandparents while Mom kept the boys, which has always perplexed me.

The way mom explained it, her ex-husband's parents desperately wanted daughters of their own; however, they never had any. So, they concocted false allegations that my mother was unfit to raise her daughters and took her to court for custody...even though they didn't seek custody of the twin boys. They felt it was their right to take Mom's children from her and fought vehemently for them until she gave in and released custody to them. Consequently, I was the only daughter Mom raised.

As it turns out, I was Mom's *get right child.* She got pregnant with me on purpose for a redux after divorcing my siblings' father, so to speak. It didn't matter if the father would be in my life; Mom just wanted me and did anything to bring me into this world - including becoming involved with a married man.

The man Mom was dating when she started having baby pangs scoffed at the idea of having a child with her, so she shifted focus to someone who wouldn't bring unnecessary drama or force himself into our lives because he was married. Well, he exceeded her expectations. He didn't even meet me until I was eight years old, leaving Mom to raise me by herself. Other than tossing her a few dollars for Christmas, my birthday and school, he did below the bare minimum for most of my life. The silent partner I never needed.

Annette Louise (James) Gaskins was my mama. And mama raised me with no assistance or interference from the outside world, just as she planned. Morals, values, behaviors, thought processes, work ethics, likes and dislikes, emotional strengths and weaknesses came from Annette. I was her shadow, glued to her side. She was extremely active in my life, committed to supporting me at school and on field trips, developing lasting friendships with my teachers, and shielding me from the world.

In the most elemental ways, I felt like Mom's creation. I thrived off her; my identity was intricately connected with hers. Even my breathing was contingent upon Mom being there. I don't remember being watched by babysitters often because she kept me with her. There were very few male companions who occupied her time; she was so leery of predators, that she didn't want a bunch of strange men around me, anyway. So, instead of relationships, I was Mom's companion, going fishing together, checking out yard sales, and helping take care of her garden. The funniest part is as much as I learned how to cultivate greenery, these days my green thumb has turned putrid orange. There was no me without Mom. Even when my teen hormones raged out of control…and I ended up pregnant.

Had Mom not sheltered me so much, maybe I would've known more about boys. She'd often say, "Don't trust what they say. You need to focus on school. That's all." She never elaborated. Instead of sitting me down to explain how one day I'd grow from hating them, to being enticed by the same things that drove me mad about them, she gave commands that I was expected to follow. How, as much as I'd want to stand by my "*no*" when the time came, parts of my body would beg me to say "*yes.*" There were no heart-to-hearts about emotions and lust. No mentions of how a single, hasty decision could alter my life. All Mom said was leave them boys alone. For me, that wasn't enough.

I listened to my body instead of Mom. Without her guidance, I ran straight into an abusive relationship, and was later blindsided by a positive pregnancy test. *Worthless, and with child.* That's how I felt. Teen girls get pregnant all the time, I was used to that. Unfortunately, I was also numb to the emotional and physical abuse at the hands of a guy who behaved as though he hated me. With my pregnancy came shame, hurt, disgust and disappointment. Funny thing is, it wasn't my growing belly or my child that were ripping me apart. Not even the loveless relationship I was in was the source of my sorrow. Mom's reaction to her baby girl having a child of her own caused my emotional downfall.

The anger seething from Mom's pores when she found out I'd been skipping school to be with this boy was worse than any punishment she could dole out. Guess my growing belly I proved everything in the dark eventually does have a light shone on it. Every day inside the confines of our own home, Mom made me feel like I failed her and the plans she had for my life. I was constantly reminded how much she'd done for me, how there was no logical explanation for my *fall from grace*. Her best backlash was reserved for me inside that house. But to those on the outside, she was my biggest supporter. It's funny how our lives can sometimes beat with two separate hearts.

The disappointment in Mom's eyes when she glanced at me was nothing compared to the way she sparred with anybody who dared to speak negatively about me and my situation. As upset as she was with me, Mom was a doting grandmother/mother to my daughter. I wouldn't have traded it for the universe. She knew I was too immature to be a mother, so after my daughter, Quiamony, was born, Mom assumed caregiving duties. Before I gave birth, it was entirely different.

A thick veil of darkness covered our home for about a year before Quiamony entered our world. Our family was existing; however, we weren't living. On the surface, everything seemed normal. But the vitality in our relationships was missing. It was something I craved and needed more than ever. My daughter's birth drove the darkness away, and restored joy to our house and family. Yet, it was still impossible for me to shake the shame and guilt. My relationship with my mother had been broken, and I slipped into depression. The feeling that I'd lost her haunted me every day – even after her death. Things weren't the same between us. I wasn't the same. I'm still not the person I was before I became a mother.

Here I was trying to adjust to having a baby, and Mom was hassling me about school. None of her other children completed high school, had decent jobs, or survived without hustling or living off public assistance, so I can see why she was so hard on me about finishing school. If I didn't graduate, then she failed to raise the perfect daughter, right? Even after proving the legacy of teen pregnancy in our family hadn't stopped with me, Mom pushed me to excel. But I didn't want to be pushed.

First of all, no grade less than an A was acceptable. So, I had to study between diaper changes and feedings. Talk about pressure! But because I managed to excel, I was in honors and advanced placement courses. Consequently, my schedule was packed. So much for having a social life. I didn't have to worry about getting a job, but I didn't have friends either. Not because friends were forbidden, but because I was introverted and Mom didn't encourage them. That left me at home with schoolwork, and a baby.

With nothing to do outside of studying and nowhere to go, I grew into a home body, which was fine with Mom. All she asked was that I excel in school. Church wasn't even a priority. It never had been. We went on special occasions, but I wasn't raised in the pews, and didn't have a connection to God. My life's blueprint was school, home, and parenting. That's it. But as long as I was with Mom, I was content. Even through the emotional distress, I still thrived off her. Without friends, Mom was enough.

…until my world crashed.

Mom smoked until I was 10 years old. Two years after my daughter was born, she was diagnosed with terminal lung cancer. For years, she had a nagging cough that she ignored. Didn't even mention it during doctor's visits. Maybe she was scared of what they'd tell her. Maybe she didn't think it was a big deal. But we noticed she was forgetting simple things and had trouble matching her thoughts with her words and pushed for her to seek help. Mom consented to go, but none of us were prepared for the diagnosis: advanced lung cancer that traveled to her brain. *Mom was going to die.*

There wasn't time to process the diagnosis before the doctors started Mom on aggressive radiation treatments. A faithful member of a church for three years prior to her diagnosis, her faith grew stronger, like she was preparing her body and soul for the next phase. Faith helped her, but I was crushed.

How can You take her away, God? She's my life!

As Mom was stripped of her ability to speak, walk and care for herself, our family became more fractured. Consumed with their own issues, my siblings weren't available to help care for Mom, leaving me to be her sole caregiver. The twins, Jay and Jack, have developmental delays which impaired their ability to help, so I don't include them. They couldn't help if they wanted to. The thing is, at 18 years old, I wasn't equipped to care for Mom effectively, professionally, or adequately either. But I was all she had. Just me. And *just me* was okay. Besides, Mom so fiercely believed God was going to heal her, I assumed the Lord would alleviate her need for me beyond my capacity of care.

Mom was diagnosed in May of 1994.

By December 17th, she was gone.

Even now, the day Mom died plays clearly in my mind. The night before, I'd left her room and had gone into mine. Holding my baby in my arms, I cried out to God, begging Him to spare her life. "I can't live without her," I screamed, "please save her!" I knew enough about God to know it was possible for Him to save her. I screamed, cried, begged, pleaded and threw myself at His mercy. As I poured out my heart, I realized only God could restore me, and heal Mom.

The next morning, I crept inside Mom's room, trying not to disturb her. Everything was so still. I didn't hear anything, with the exception of her coughing and gasping, an excruciating rattle barreling from her chest. *This is the end.* I knew it was over, but I felt her fighting. Something deep in my soul suggested the fight wasn't for herself, it was for me and Quiamony. Mom never cared enough about herself to put herself first. No matter what the relationship was, she chose others over herself; that's the kind of woman she was. A fighter. Even if the fight wasn't for her own victory.

Both of us seemed to know her fate was sealed, but didn't want to admit it. Mom desired to do right by me and help me to be better than the woman she was. I saw it in her face as she gasped for air. She never had to say a word, even if she was able to. She was content to go, but I knew she wanted to stay. For me. That's why I did something that I regretted for many years afterwards.

I made the decision to free us both.

I saw my mother for who she was. The pain she was enduring for me shone through her hollow eyes. Finally realized that I wasn't the disappointment I thought she saw me as, I was the reflection of what Mom thought about herself. The curse she failed to break. Listening to her breath become more labored, her eyes growing lifeless, I knew I couldn't allow Mom to suffer out of concern for *perfecting* me. Watching her die was my discovery that I could survive. I didn't know how, but I knew I would. I had to set both of us free.

Mom laid in bed, wreathing in pain. I leaned over her body and wrapped my arms around her. Then I gently rested my head on her chest, and whispered, "Mama, I love you. If you are fighting for yourself, keep fighting. But if you're fighting for me and Quiamony, don't. We'll be okay."

I sealed my promise with a kiss. Then waited for God's will to be done.

A few minutes later, the hospice nurse I'd called arrived. I left her alone to examine Mom, as I busied myself with other things. Shortly after going in to see her, the nurse emerged from Mom's room, nonchalantly informing me, "She's dying today."

Everything else the nurse said about next steps were words without sound. Her lips moved, but I didn't hear anything. *Mom's leaving me NOW.* As much as I'd done to prepare for this moment, I wasn't ready. How can anyone ever be ready to let go of their lifeline?

Once the nurse left, my sisters rushed into the house, praying to every god they knew to save Mom. Somehow, they managed to find time in between prayers to criticize me for Mom's Depends not being changed. "Her bedding's wet," they complained. They would've kept going if the ambulance didn't arrive to take Mom to the ER. One hour after our talk, Mom was gone. I was gone, too. I instantly hated myself for giving her permission to die. It was guilt that would keep a chokehold on me for years to come. Suddenly, I no longer existed. *How do I live without her?* She was MY EVERYTHING.

I wanted to snatch my words to Mom back. Pretend they'd never come out of my mouth. Maybe if I hadn't said anything, she'd still be alive. I believed I unjustly used my power to manipulate a situation that wasn't meant for me to control. For years, that conversation sat in my throat like vomit that wouldn't spew. If I hadn't released her, Mom would've fought and survived. That *god complex* quietly dwelling in each of us revealed itself through me in the ugliest way. And it cost the person I loved most. I should've silenced the inner voice saying, *"If I just pray enough, think or speak it into existence, or wish hard enough whatever I want will magically happen."* The voice was wrong. Dead wrong.

In truth, only God has the power I thought I exercised. Still, granting Mom the permission to give up almost drug me to the grave with her. Who was I to take away her will to fight? Who was I not to fight alongside her, just as hard as she was? Who was I to sign the separation papers? That couldn't be love, could it? It took years and a load of therapy to finally realize my actions were the very epitome of *love*. Love is knowing when it's time to let go. Love is considering someone else's feelings and needs apart from your own. Love is doing the right thing regardless of potential hurt and trauma. Yes, I did the right thing because I loved my mama.

So, what I said remains true: *My mother's death was the best thing that has ever happened to me.* Had she lived, the person I've become wouldn't exist. The experiences, wisdom, lessons, joy, pain, trauma, joy, and successes I've experienced wouldn't have happened with her alive. Upholding her as my god would've held me back from my purpose. But when she died, first I had to deal with the void left by her absence.

CHAPTER 2

The Months After

Following Mom's death, the days, weeks, and months were pure hell. Outwardly I was functioning, but I'd internally shut down. Inconsistently eating, sleeping, and managing daily care. Suddenly, walking, breathing, and even blinking morphed into mountains I was forced to climb. *You don't have to fight, Mom.* That's what I told her. And that's how I lost my will to fight for myself.

Don't get me wrong – every decision others made for me while I was in a state of confusion were welcome luxuries. Besides, I was all out of options, and couldn't find joy in anything. My happy places, like learning history, playing with my daughter, or simply chatting with friends and neighbors lost their spark. Once again, I was living in a world devoid of color or vitality, much the way life was prior to Quiamony's birth. Grief heavier than anything I could ever imagine engulfed my family. For me, it was like a weighted blanket that was too heavy to comfort me. My intense, emotional response to my first crisis found me unable to function. Mom's death was trying to kill me. Which I would've been fine with (because at least I would've been with her), but considering my daughter prevented me from doing anything crazy.

It wasn't long before my relatives descended upon the house where the twins and my oldest brother, Brian also lived. Several of Mom's siblings and her father came ahead of the funeral to help with arrangements, which was overwhelming because everyone wanted *something*. My uncle, Rob, wanted my mother's gold bell she used to summon us when she needed something. Her friends wanted articles of clothing as keepsakes. Others wanted trinkets that meant a lot to her. And *everyone* wanted a hand in making decisions about the funeral. I wished I could slap a *cease-and-desist* on all of it, along with a muzzle on their mouths.

Because I was the financially responsible party, it was my duty to bear the brunt of Mom's funeral expenses. Thankfully, she was a forward thinker, and had obtained several life insurance policies where I was named sole beneficiary. When the question came up as to why, Mom explained to my sister, Grace, that since my father wasn't around, once she was gone, I essentially had no one outside of a toddler who depended on me. Her answer didn't sit well with some my siblings, but that's the way things were.

It should've been an honor to take care of Mom's affairs, but I was numb. Didn't feel a thing. If I could just go to sleep for a month, maybe the pain would float away. Unfortunately, life doesn't work that way. I was the beneficiary, and nothing happened without my approval.

The outfit Mom would be buried in, her coffin...all the tedious things necessary to host a proper homegoing service. Sole responsibility fell on me.

One day, my siblings and I were in a heated debate over the burial clothes I'd selected for Mom. See, two weeks before she passed, I'd gone to JC Penney, aimlessly walking the aisles in search of the perfect Christmas gift befitting a queen. I settled on a beautiful, long-sleeved silk night gown for her to open on Christmas day. I just knew she'd be thrilled at the time and care I took in picking something so exquisite out for her. She was always so focused on meeting our needs and making sure we were happy, Mom never bought anything for herself. She deserved something brand new, that no one else had owned, and didn't come from the thrift store. I was so excited to give it to her, I could barely contain myself.

Sadly, the wonderful Christmas morning I planned wasn't meant to be. Because Mom died, I'd never have the chance to see her reaction to her special gift. But it was hers, and I wanted her to wear it. Besides, it was perfect, and met the funeral home's dress code.

My siblings had a different idea. They accused me of dishonoring our mother's memory with such a *tacky* choice. They saw it as sleepwear; I saw it as something special she deserved. I respected us making joint decisions as her children, because I didn't want to make them alone. As much as it broke my heart to do it, I gave in and accompanied my siblings in search of more *appropriate* attire.

While we were out shopping, my overwhelming desire to dress Mom in that gown intensified. After we rummaged through the third store, I explained to my siblings why I'd chosen that gown. It represented my love and appreciation for Mom. Eventually, they relented, giving me a small glimpse of peace.

That fire was squelched, but the peace was temporary. Once the family gathered at the funeral home to complete final arrangements, tensions rose. Everyone had their own ideas about what would be befitting of our queen. Decisions about the casket, vault, limo, location, burial time and everything essential to making the day memorable morphed into battles. Given the high expenses of funerals, I was focused on making choices that were beautiful, yet economically sound. Mom used to say, "It doesn't make sense spending all that money on a box that's going in the ground." So, her wants overrode everyone's input in my ear.

There were too many family members who weren't putting a dime on Mom's funeral, yet had plenty to say about sparing no expense for it. They pressed so hard, I lost it inside. No, really – I LOST it. I was tired, drained and over it all. Just as I was about to explode on everyone, Uncle Rob spoke up, reminding my family that the final decision was mine to make. "You choose what you feel would be befitting," he told me after he hushed them. Then, I took a deep breath, and decided what I wanted my queen to have.

An elegant, white-pearl casket, interior doused on Mom's favorite color, blue. Her gown was eggshell and adorned with pearl accents. The perfect combination of Mom's regal class. In the end, it was simple and elegant - a funeral my mother would have been proud of. I was proud, too.

The thing to remember is that grief doesn't disappear when the casket's lowered in the ground. And it doesn't last a week or two, which is exactly how long the support lasts once the repast is over. The food, cards, and money stops. The crowd's gone. House is quiet. The reality of the loss settles in. That reality descended upon my family like a category five hurricane.

Christmas day was looming, but the remnants of the funeral lingered. I was a hot mess. I don't remember Christmas or the days following Mom's death with clarity. Some snatches of time were captured on film, kept for us to remember; however, the one thing I do remember was how my siblings and I initially handled our loss.

Our *new normal* was difficult to adjust to for me and my siblings. I was so angry at my sister Linda for not coming home after she was released from her own hospitalization, knowing the grave condition mom was in. She knew Mom's health was getting worse, but she dwelled on their fractured relationship instead of being committed to the woman who gave her life. She gave up on Mom and cast her aside.

When she finally showed up, my sister was devastated. My mother was her safety net. No matter how hard they battled, my sister knew Mom would never forsake or see her go without. So, as I witnessed her breaking down, I yelled, "Swallow your tears! Nobody wants to hear you crying!"

Of course, I was in my feelings, but my sympathy for my sister had dwindled to nothing. Still, no one has the right to tell us how to grieve. Regardless of the state of the relationship, grief is real. We have the right to grieve how we need to, without judgement or interference from others. As much as I'd like to say I apologized for my actions that day, I'd be lying. Linda's lifestyle and current state of mind have made it impossible for her to receive an apology from me, even if I offered it. Maybe one day we'll reconcile, but it's highly unlikely.

Then there's Brian. The cunning one. Although he lived with us, he didn't financially contribute to household expenses. Even when Mom was alive, he was reluctant to offer any tangible support because he wasn't expected to. However, when she died, he grieved hard, crying when he thought no one was looking. I remember keeping a particular song on repeat that talked about losing a mother. My brother asked me not to play it again; it was too overwhelming. It was soothing to me, but I obliged him, anyway.

Adding to our stress, Jack kept running away to the cemetery where Mom was buried. I suspect he was looking for her, thinking she was coming back. As he ran away, Jay isolated himself and stayed busy with work. Grace maintained a smooth façade but was just as shattered as I was inside. What I loved so much was the fact that even in the midst of dealing with her sadness, Grace supported me. After all, I was the youngest, least experienced, and the most gullible of us. Grace looked out for me, which still means the world.

The way I dealt with grief would make a therapist cringe. In no way did he deserve it, but after Mom died, I needed somewhere to pour my love, so I sank everything I had into my boyfriend. The infidelity, lies, selfishness, and blatant disregard for my wellbeing…I ignored how he treated me in the name of *love*. He was the male figure I needed in the absence of my father; when I got pregnant by him, I figured my baby was going to need him, too.

That man didn't love me. I don't know why I ever thought he was ready to be a father. It wasn't even a shock when he tried to get me to abort my baby. The relationship (if that's what you want to call it) went well past its expiration date; however, I wanted to give my new baby a father, since Quiamony didn't have one. I failed again. Staring down the face of single motherhood with trepidation. But if my mother could raise her children alone, I could do the same for mine.

Mom's death. Family falling apart. Pregnant and alone, again. It was like all of these situations were stuffed in a glass bottle that was about to shatter. I ended up going against many therapists' advice and made a life-changing decision in the midst of grieving: I took off to another city, because there were too many reminders of Mom in my hometown. Her scent was there. Her essence. Every memory of her was wrapped around my aching heart. It was too much for my peace and sanity. So, I ran. Away from the pain, the people, and emotional turmoil. The only way for to escape the grief demons was to get away from them. Had I been able to identify the emotional crisis I was experiencing, things would have been different. But I truly believed I was deemed to live in torment for the rest of my life.

Unaddressed grief turns into self-imposed anguish. Nothing was more important to me than wallowing in it. Did I want to die? No. But I was awful close. My only defense against suicide were Quiamony and the precious baby in my womb, Kesiara. They kept me focused. They were my *WHY*. I had to live for them.

Mom had left me enough money to survive until I found a job to keep us stable, so financially, we'd be alright for a short while. There was a great apartment I found one city over, so I packed up Quiamony and invited Jay, to move in with us. He needed someone to look after him. I didn't even tell anyone we were leaving until a week before the move.

By now, Jack was living in a group home. He was put there for running away so much. Truth is, at 18, I wasn't equipped to care for anyone who had the mental and physical health challenges Jack did. I was still a kid, struggling to raise my own child. My older siblings should've stepped up to help take care of Jack. *He's your brother too*, I wanted to scream in their faces. They saw me screwing up, and still did nothing to help take care of and keep him in our home. They didn't even help make sure Mom had adequate healthcare, either. And I resented it. As angry as I was, I did what I could to take care of Mom. And as far as Jack was concerned, we didn't receive state assistance. However, when the situation spun out of control, the state intervened and placed him in a safe environment. Finally, I was free to focus on what I wanted… running away.

So, I did.

The funny thing is, no matter how hard we sprint towards the finish line, grief can't be outrun. Really, when it comes to grief, there is no finish line. I thought relocating to a new environment would help me get past the pain, but being sequestered in the new place was just as agonizing. Empty, alone, worn out. Sobbing uncontrollably at random times. The days slowly crept by, making me sadder. It seemed like I would never be happy again.

My brother was just as distressed as I was. We were empty shells, moving around in a daze. As a photographer, Jay's way of grieving was taking countless photos at the funeral. He framed a poster-sized photo of Mom in her casket and hung it in his room - an open space in the middle of the apartment, which forced me to relive Mom's death every day. That photo was a glaring reminder that she was gone. Seeing her face as soon as I walked in the door made me feel like she was dying over and over again and taking me with her. It constantly reopened the wound I needed so desperately to heal. I was afraid to ask my brother to take the poster down, but it was beating me down so badly, I knew it couldn't stay. So, I begged my mother's best friend, Aunt Liv, to ask him to do it for me; it disappeared shortly after. I was relieved, but still had to face a glaring truth: Grief had claimed my clarity.

Removing the photo didn't have the effect I thought it would. My mind still swirled with doubt and self-persecution. *If I hadn't told Mom she could die, she'd still be here*, I repeated to myself over and over. No one knew what I had done. If I ever told my siblings, they'd hate me, so I kept it to myself. Resigned to be alone forever because I assumed there was no way any man would want someone as messed up as me, imagine how shocked I was when I met my future husband.

They're Gone! Now What?

I rushed to move in with him, but now I realize the move was divine. On paper, he didn't check all the boxes. Especially the fact he was 12 years older and married. Separated, but married. Naturally, everyone thought I was crazy for being with a married man who was so much older. Had I known what I know now, I probably would've waited to get involved with him.

…and I would've missed out on one of the most important relationships of my life.

I should've been happy by that time, but happiness didn't feel right. Like I didn't deserve it. Good people didn't need to be around me because I'd only disappoint them. After all, hadn't I disappointed Mom? So, I slid beneath the weighted blanket (burdens), where torturing myself felt plush and easy. Despair and loneliness were my security; I didn't need better. And I didn't deserve it.

Many years later, as an undergraduate at Norfolk State University, I was introduced to theorist Dr. Elizabeth Kubler-Ross, who specialized in death and dying; however, she's most widely known for her grief model. According to the Kubler-Ross model, there are five stages to the grief process: denial, anger, bargaining, depression, and acceptance. Each stage isn't linear, meaning they don't occur in order, and not everyone experiences all of them. As Dr. Kubler-Ross puts it, grief doesn't have a time limit - it takes as long as it takes. Studying her model in undergrad prompted me to explore how I was grieving. Mom had been gone eleven years, but the model helped me discover that I was still in crisis.

Dr. Kubler-Ross' position that grief is normal and individualistic, spoke to me. When someone we love dies, families either pull together or fall apart. My family dealt with grief privately and fell apart. Mom was the literal glue that held us together. She smoothed over fights and made it her mission for us to get along. Most of my siblings formed bonds that remain today, but not with me. They bullied me, whether it was due to my being the baby, or resenting the attention I got from Mom. I'll probably never know for sure. But the bond between my siblings and me was severed long before Annette died. 27 years later, some of us still have yet to accept that she's gone.

Today, I am a licensed clinical social worker, with an emphasis on mental wellness. For the past nine years I've worked with clients who struggle with a myriad of mental health issues, including grief. Grief is typically triggered by an abrupt life change, which renders survivors unstable to the point where they are unbalanced and functionally impaired. In essence, this loss or life change forces the bereaved to adapt to a new life without their loved one. Although their essence remains, the void they leave behind is glaring. One moment, they're breathing—the next, those they left behind are a withering mess.

CHAPTER 3

Beaten Down

I don't remember what happened in the world when Mom died. It was like everything stopped. While contemplating writing this book, out of curiosity, I Googled events, music, and sports, searching for anything of significance that happened in December 1994. Turns out, I missed a lot: a subway bombing in New York City, the standoff between baseball players and owners over a salary cap, the discovery of a galaxy 15 billion light years away from earth, and an earthquake killing over 5,000 people in Japan. I even missed the number one song topping the charts that year— "On Bended Knee" by Boyz II Men. Seeing how much I'd missed revealed the biggest smack in the face. Life keeps moving, whether we want it to or not.

The death of a loved one doesn't place life on pause. Bills still need to be paid, children need care, and spouses require attention. Not to mention maintaining our jobs, fulfilling responsibilities and doing basic things to survive, such as eating and sleeping. No matter how we feel, we still have to engage with the world, in spite of the allure isolation may have. Life continues on, spinning like we're a plate spinner, struggling to keep every plate in rotation on a thin stick. If we're not careful, the slightest misstep will shatter us into a million shards of ceramic on the ground, and we're still expected to go on. I suffered my greatest loss, yet I was expected to go on.

The more life happened, the further I withdrew. Various mini crises popped up all around me, but all I could focus on was living without my mother. Like when two days after Mom passed, Quiamony was admitted to Children's Hospital of the King's Daughters for eczema and asthma, illnesses she's struggled with since she was four months old. Before she died, Mom and I struggled to find her adequate treatment; the CHKD doctors proved to be lifesavers. For those who don't know, eczema is another name for *atopic dermatitis*. It usually develops in early childhood, manifesting as an inflamed, crusty, thick, scaly rash, which leads to itching, burning and sometimes infection. Due to her chronic symptoms, Quiamony was taking various topical medications and antihistamines for itching, but it was ineffective. Her natural instinct was to scratch, which led to the horrible skin infection that landed her in the hospital, where she stayed until the day before Christmas - two days after the funeral.

Mom, I just lost you, I can't lose my baby girl, too!

My days were spent handling funeral arrangements, nights were spent in the hospital watching, caring and praying for my daughter. Her biological father visited her once, but he wasn't supportive at all, leaving me alone at her bedside, stressed and too afraid to sleep. Making sure she was still breathing wasn't my only concern; every time I closed my eyes, Mom invaded my dreams. Ghosts terrified me. They still do today. However, these days my prayer life is so powerful, I know how to contend with them. Was I being irrational back then? Probably. At least Kesiara's father spent nights on the phone with me as long as he could, which made me feel a bit less anxious.

Around this time, I saw how much damage my father's absence had done to my emotional health. Even Mom's ex-husband attended her funeral, in support of the four children they had together. My father wasn't there. "*Who's going to hold me or give me comfort?*" I thought. Of course, Aunt Liv was there to console me, but that only amplified my father's absence even more.

The day after the funeral, he showed up at the house. "Why weren't you there for me?" I asked him. His excuse made me sick to my stomach. Claimed his cousin was in the hospital in Richmond and needed him. "*But I needed you,*" I wanted to scream. Instead of telling him, I swallowed my disappointment. There was no point in telling him how I felt; he'd never understand. After we parted ways, I ended up doing what I always do: crawled under my *weighted blanket,* asking myself, *"Why don't I deserve anyone to love me?"*

In the days leading up to my move, I realized that my relationship with my unborn child's father was coming to an end. There'd already been major signs the breakup was coming, but I ignored them. His infidelity, egotistical, deceiving, and calculating behavior stressed me out even more than I was already. *"Am I in this thing alone?"* I wondered.

Reflecting on our time together, there were so many disappointments. Things like attending prom, double dating with peers, going to the movies, lounging at the beach, or dancing at the hottest teen clubs—we didn't make those kinds of memories together. All we did was hang at my house, watching television. His ambivalence towards me was too much, and I had enough. The day after I moved, I broke up with him.

In the midst of everything else falling apart, I had to figure out how to manage the house Mom left behind. Being diagnosed with a mental illness when I was six months old had forced her to retire from the shipyard. For as long as I can remember, we survived off her fixed income, which included disability benefits from Jack. Eventually, Jay secured a job and started helping her with expenses, but it wasn't much. I don't know how, but Mom made paying bills, buying groceries, and providing for us seem effortless. I wish it was that way for me.

I was totally unprepared for adult life. It took a while, but I was able to learn how to balance a checkbook and cook. Then I started paying a little on all my bills each month; however, what I put in never seemed to be enough, even with Jay's help. Disconnection notices piled up faster than we could get the money to stop them. Telephone, electricity, water. Everything was shut off at one time or another.

The mountains were moving in front of me instead of out of my way. Not having a driver's license was one of the biggest hurdles. Financially supporting my daughter was another. It was hard finding someone to take me to appointments or run errands, and I didn't want to rely on public assistance, because the social services system disturbed my peace of mind. I was afraid to drive so obtaining my license didn't happen for several years. Friends of my mother and my sister Grace served as my main forms of transportation for several months.

Before she died, Mom helped me apply for AFDC (Aid to Families with Dependent Children) and food stamps when I turned 18. The intrusive questions and looks of disdain from the employees during the application process reeked of me being beneath them. They were so nasty, I vowed never to ask anyone for help again. If it meant I would be humiliated that way again, they could keep it. No more public assistance, ever again in my life. I was grateful that the money from Mom's insurance policies got me off assistance and sustained me for a year. It was my intent to get a job but childcare is expensive so I made the decision to stay at home for a while. I was close to giving up.

"God, help me! When will it stop? Haven't I suffered enough? Can't You just wake me up from this nightmare and let Mom be there to take care of everything like she used to?" I was so angry with God, I didn't bother actually asking Him any of those things. I blamed Him. All of this was His fault.

The last thing I needed to deal with was everyone having something to say about how I was caring for my child, how I took care of Mom before she died, how I cared for my brother and my niece, Tracy, (who lived with us until November 1994), and how I chose to *turn my back on the family* and move to another city, but they did. I couldn't take it anymore. There was no escape from the world crumbling on top of me. All I could do was brace myself for the abuse, judgement, pain, sadness, loneliness, and emptiness.

As I took it all in, time moved on without my connecting dejection to grief. The symptoms were clear, but not to me. It wasn't until years later that the reason I felt off was because when we don't earnestly deal with grief head on, grief will most certainly deal with us.

CHAPTER 4

Memory Lapse

My body, mind, and spirit were inundated with more than they could handle. Life took a toll on me. I'd withdrawn to myself and lacked the ability to notice the bizarre changes in and around me. It took the Pandemic of 2020 for me to realize what happened to me from 1994-1995.

When I sat down to write this book, I discovered how my brain protected me by blocking out multiple events and timeframes. Professionals call this *dissociation*. Dissociation is the disconnection or separation of one thing from another. The mind blots out information regarding traumatic or stressful events in order to protect its host, impacting their thoughts, feelings, surroundings, and memories. In extreme cases, identities and time perception are adversely affected, too. These symptoms usually resolve themselves once the circumstances pass, but more stressful situations may trigger more severe mental health disruptions and large lapses of time.

Reflecting on that period in my life, what stands out is how I was unable to chronologically sort out timelines and arrange them in order. It was infuriating! For instance, I discovered things I thought took place around the same time Mom died actually occurred months or years later. Then there's how I inadvertently grouped my second pregnancy, the move to Norfolk, and the conflicts with my siblings together. In my mind, I was pregnant before my mother died, when in reality, I didn't get pregnant until a month after she was gone. I ended up shifting the move and family fights to wherever my mind wanted them to fit on the timeline, and was too exhausted to figure out if it was right.

These days I understand the shuffling was my mind's way of protecting me because I was extremely vulnerable. But it's fascinating how complex and advanced our brains are to conceptualize emotional shields the way it does. I've heard about the brain dissociating from abuse, like billionaire Tyler Perry talking of visualizing himself in his favorite place when his father was physically punishing him. He's not the only one I'd heard mention this, but I never considered how subtle our minds are in protecting us from what we've endured. The protection covering me in 2020 is the same I had in 1995. I didn't realize how much I needed it.

The pandemic of 2020 brought on similar symptoms I'd experienced in the past. It wasn't until 2021 that I noticed I was confusing things from 2019 with those in 2020. I said things like, *"Oh, we were on the cruise last year,"* or *"Her graduation party was last year,"* unaware what I thought were months was really a year that had gone by. It became clear that my mind blocked all of 2020 from my memory. I worked, started grad school, managed my home, strengthened my connection with God and became increasingly active in my church, but my mind failed to hold onto the memories regarding the time/space continuum. Those things I did remember, weren't in the right time, almost as if 2020 didn't exist. I skipped from 2019 to 2021. Everything was there, except the right time.

On top of dissociation, my anxiety shot through the roof. There's always been this undercurrent of worry within me; not remembering things the way I should made it worse. Mom definitely passed on the gift of worrying from herself to me. She toiled over us, her friends, other family members, and being able to provide. If Mom could find something to worry about, she did, without trying to hide it. That's how she ended up passing down her anxiousness to me. She wouldn't even rest easy until I got safely home from school. It was tiresome, but her fussing was a reminder that she cared.

There's one moment that really stands out for me. Mom went on an all-night fishing trip without letting me – her shadow, know she was going. "Mom," I yelled when I got home from school, "Mom?"

When she didn't answer, I went straight into a panic. She was perfectly fine, but to me, Mom was missing. I don't know how long I peered out the window waiting for her, beads of sweat tracing down my face. We didn't have cell phones back then, so it wasn't like I could just call to find out where she was. I conjured up all sorts of gruesome scenarios about what could've happened to her, until my head ached. By the time Mom walked through the front door the next day, I was a wreck. Questioned her like she was my child rather than the other way around. Now my mama didn't play or tolerate disrespect, but I didn't care. I lit straight into her for worrying me the way she had. Of course, she was all over me about getting out of pocket with her, but I was prepared for any punishment she doled out, as long as she heard me.

Mom's death was the sum of every fear I'd ever had about losing her. I spent my childhood being afraid that she was going to die, which came true by my late teens. All of that worrying spilled right over from me to my daughters. I was hyperaware of everything involving my girls and kept them close to me. The only babysitter I used was Jay, and he barely made the cut. Playing could cause them to injure themselves, so I was extra careful about that. Everywhere my girls were, I was, too. Creating a safe place for us pushed grief, depression, and incompleteness aside. My children became *my safe place*. And I was content to stay there.

The same way my mother was my shield, I was fierce about protecting my daughters. I didn't want them to feel exposed to danger, the way I did when Mom died. *Who will protect me now?* Considering my inexperience, I was clueless how to handle all the attention I got from men, especial several married ones in the community. Instead of standing my ground and chasing them away, I kept thinking, "*If Mom was alive, she'd protect me from them.*" In some twisted way, I believe when she died, they saw their opportunity to take advantage of my innocence and exploit my naiveté. These seasoned men were chasing after a vulnerable young girl, and it wasn't right. It still creeps me out how they slithered around me, pretending to show compassion for my loss. I was already anxious; those creeps had me frantic.

Warding off strange men wasn't the only new problem I was dealing with. I hadn't put much thought into how the body and soul react to death. Before death hit my house, I was able to attend funerals, view the bodies, and support the bereaved with ease, if you can call any of the components of death easy. Losing Mom turned nonchalance into panic. Leaving her in the hospital that final time provoked my aversion to anything dealing with death or dying. Especially, the business end of dying.

Part of my duties as Mom's beneficiary included approving her appearance prior to the wake. I was expected to inspect the mortician's work on Mom's corpse before the service, but I couldn't drag myself in the room with her body. The casket, her nails, hair, makeup, dress. It was too much. I was afraid to see her that way. So I froze outside the room, unable to go in and see my hero for the last time.

Seeing her that way meant...she was really gone. Forever. "Can you do it?" I asked Grace once I snapped out of my trance. Without hesitation, she went in and did what needed to be done to give final approval.

Just like that, I stopped attending funerals and wakes. No longer comforted the bereaved. They'd have to deal with death on their own. Suddenly, dead bodies gave me nightmares, and I didn't want to have to defend myself against their ghosts. It may sound crazy, but I was convinced that by looking at a corpse, that person's soul would attach to me. That's how anxiety works. It's irrational, intrusive, and never convenient. Since my protector was gone, I had to protect myself.

The minute I knew someone had experienced loss, I shut down and refused to talk to them about it. Why? Because loss doesn't teach us what to say, you know? I absolutely hated how awkward it was to stand there while people grasped for something to say in order to make me feel better when Mom died. What was there to say to help me *get over* my loss?

"I'm so sorry."
"It will get better."
"She's in a better place."

...or my favorite, *"I know exactly how you feel."*

Shut up! How dare you pretend to know how I FEEL. You don't know the first thing about what I'm feeling right now! All I ever managed to respond with was a hollow, "*Thank you.*"

Even if they lost their mother when they were 18 and had the exact same experiences as I had growing up, no one could've possibly known *exactly how I felt*, because they weren't me. And I'm not anybody else, so when someone told me they lost a loved one, I tended to remain silent. Mostly because a few of my relationships were already fractured from me not responding to grieving friends the way they wanted me to. I'll admit, I wasn't as supportive as I should've been. Now that I've matured, I support a person's loss with my presence, rather than coming up with empty words that won't help. What I've learned during my grief journey is that our presence is the best way to show our support.

The most glaring, confusing symptom of depression I was experiencing at this time was anger. Every day was filled with rage; I constantly teetered on the brink of explosion if someone pressed the right button. Anger is a secondary emotion, fueled by other emotions, like love. Tina Turner sang, "What's love got to do with it? Love is a secondary emotion." Outside influences drive love. It doesn't happen without another emotion coming before it, the same as anger.

No one is angry because they are *angry*. Disappointment, hurt, or sadness could be the driving forces behind it. Years ago, I was angry with everyone, including God. I was angry with Him because He betrayed me by taking my mother away. I was angry with my friends whose parents were still alive. I was angry with my siblings because unlike me, they had other family members who supported them. I was angry with the world, because the world couldn't feel the pain I was feeling. Most of all, I was angry with myself for hurting and being unable to function without falling apart.

I was a ball of rage, slowly coming apart. Watching others prancing around like they didn't have a care in the world was infuriating. I wanted to snatch the smiles off their faces. The slightest things agitated my spirit without me having an outlet to release it. As the pressure mounted, I held onto everything that was hurting me.

CHAPTER 5

Compounded Loss

December 17, 1994. The beginning of a seemingly endless stream of death, separation, and abandonment. I was losing everything and delving deeper into darkness.

Grief is often associated with loss; however, relationships, jobs, titles, locations, or personality changes are losses, too. It's possible to grieve someone who's still alive. Any person, animal, thing, or idea that has been removed from our presence initiates grief. Mom's death was the catalyst for many other significant losses to come and shaped how I'd deal with loss in the future.

The next major loss I experienced after Mom was ending the relationship with my boyfriend. Don't get me wrong – ending the relationship was the best thing to do, but that didn't stop me from missing his companionship. At least I no longer had to stress over where he was, what he was doing, who he was with, question how he felt about me or if he was going to break up with me for someone else. I was physically free, but my mind was still bound.

That relationship had me in a constant state of frustration. I got so used to the stress from it, I failed to recognize the catatonic state I was in once the relationship ended. There was even a time when I completely broke down because I was pregnant, couldn't make the one-sided relationship work, and was about to birth another child whose father wouldn't be around. I was following in my mother's footsteps and noticed many other women on the same path. I failed to provide a different future for my children.

Moving away from my siblings tore us further apart. Growing up, I remember Mom making every possible effort to stay connected to her family. She craved family bonds and worked hard to help form them between me and my siblings, but it never happened.

During the 1940s and 1950s, many African Americans migrated north from the Deep South in search of prosperity. My maternal grandfather was among them. When Mom was extremely young, he abandoned her and my grandmother in Georgia for a better life in Detroit with his sister. Over time he remarried and started a new family, so my grandmother did, too. Mom lived most of her childhood as an only child. I don't recall her telling me she visited her father after he left, only that she briefly lived with him following my grandmother's death. I believe she wanted to stay connected with him, but I'm just speculating. What I do know is, Mom passed her craving for family togetherness along to me.

They're Gone! Now What?

We often call mothers and grandmothers the *glue that holds the family together.* That's so true about Mom. She wanted her children to get along and love each other and wouldn't tolerate us fighting. It got to where I wouldn't tell her when they were bullying me, because I didn't want to be a tattletale (even though I did cry to her often). Mom was a peacekeeper; when she died, the glue no longer stuck.

Moving to Norfolk caused me to lose my grip on the family I had left. Drifting away from each other was exactly the opposite of what Mom wanted. Most of my siblings had no transportation, and our communication was severely limited. As time went on, Grace and Kerry, my other sister, went silent on me. As much as I'd like to place the sole blame on them, an equal share of that responsibility belongs to me. Even worse, I don't regret it. The truth is, my siblings, exes, and even my mother weren't meant to be included in the next chapter of my life. It was destiny for them to leave, even if I wasn't thrilled with the means of departure.

In addition to the people, I lost my community: my neighborhood. I moved into my childhood home at five-years-old. My great-grandfather's house. There, I was part of the Black, working class community; the neighborhood was a part of me. Everyone knew, talked to, visited and helped one another. The essence of what community's all about. With the exception of one other house on the block,

Mom's house was the only one with children. The rest of the residents were older, established married couples. Some had grandchildren that I played with, but most were just working folks who enjoyed our community as much as I did.

My house was the one all the kids wanted to play at. It sat on two lots, and there was plenty of space for us to get into whatever we wanted. No one worried about kids playing outside alone like we do today. All we knew was the sun felt good, we had all the space in the world and had loads of fun. From May until September every year, Mom hosted the most fabulous cookouts. They were always a grand affair, with card games, delicious food, drinks, music and enjoying one another. Prentis Park in Portsmouth was so special to me, leaving there felt like another death.

I wanted a clean break from my past, but I was totally isolated at my new place. There were a few neighbors I met, but they didn't compare to the ones I had back home. The neighborhood history was foreign to me, I wasn't familiar with the hangouts or where to get the best Chinese food. I didn't have a clue what my neighbors' names were. So many unknowns had me depressed again. For a while, I visited my old neighborhood to see the woman I was named after and to enjoy the sounds and smells radiating from the block. Then, before I realized it, a year passed without me going back. Then another ten. Eventually, I accepted that I was no longer part of that community. And it hurt.

Who am I if I'm not Mavis Gaskins from Des Moines Avenue?

About a year ago, I went back to the neighborhood to take Quiamony to get her hair braided. Driving past the space where my old house used to be, I noticed it had been torn down and replaced by two single family dwellings. They're beautiful, but they're not *home*. The entire block looked different. Many of my old neighbors have passed away, new families have moved in, and the smells and sounds of the block have faded into the recesses of my memory. Most shocking is how small the block has become. As a child, it looked bigger than life. As an adult, it's almost insignificant. A reminder that I'm no longer a member of the community.

Of all the losses I've endured, losing myself has been the most impactful. When Mom died, my identity passed away, too. *Who am I without her?*

I questioned my worth, my ability to take care of me and my children, and my ability to love and be loved. Doubted my ability to parent. *Will I be a good mother? Can my children count on me to care for them? Will I be as restrictive as my own mother? Will I be able to marry a good man so that they can have a father?*

All my life, my family told me I needed to be smart, because I wasn't pretty enough to get married or have children. Coincidently, I'm the only one who's married, with the most children. Life's funny that way. I really believed them when they told me that. They crushed my self-esteem. They were the ones who were supposed to be my safe place. The ones who loved their little sister enough to protect her from the world. Instead, they handed me over to it.

With Mom gone, it was clear I didn't have any emotional support. I never really trusted my siblings much, anyway. They didn't gang up on me, but it sure felt like it. They made me feel like God dropped me on the wrong doorstep because I didn't fit in with them, no matter how hard I tried. As adults, any show of support from them seems fake. In the back of my mind, they've been waiting for my downfall. Of course, this isn't true for *some* of them, but a few still ridicule and try to make me feel bad about what I'm doing with my life. Do I defend myself? Yes. But it took a long time to get to the point where I know who I am without aimlessly wandering through life, hoping not to screw things up.

Losing so much made me feel abandoned, but that was nothing new. I was always alone. Alone with my thoughts, fears, hopes and dreams buried deep inside. My mother was dead. My father didn't want me. My siblings didn't want me in their lives, and I couldn't see my own worth. So many nights, I cried myself to sleep, with no one to lean on for help. Anger was the mask to hide the fragile little girl inside. My throat was hoarse from screaming, eyes scarlet from crying, and no one heard me. Because no one was around.

CHAPTER 6

Conflicting Faith

Evangelical Pastor Rick Warren once said, "*You never know God is all you need until God is all you have.*"

At 19, I had no idea what I needed, but I knew I needed something. I was too fragile to trust anyone, and was constantly on guard, waiting for the next person to exit my life. So, I protected myself by shutting out anyone I thought would hurt me. I did have one friend, but her faith and commitment to God nearly drove me away. Faith was a bitter reminder of Mom; I didn't want to entertain it.

As I drowned in the pain, I kept searching for something to attach myself to. Everywhere I turned pushed me further into seclusion. Having so many adult responsibilities kept me from engaging in normal teenage activities. No partying, clubbing, college, or hanging out. All I had to look forward to was taking care of the child I already had and the one on the way. I had absolutely no one – not even romantic prospects. God wasn't an option because I didn't trust Him. Our relationship was conflicting. The harder I tried to run from Him, the more I wanted to cling to Him.

I wondered why I wasn't raised in church. Mom occasionally sent me, my brothers and nephew, Drew, to a predominately white church in Portsmouth, but that was the extent of our religious experience. For a year, she consistently tossed us on the bus, but only went herself when my nephew and Jay and Jack were baptized. Then there was the summer we went to vacation Bible school at a black church, but we weren't members anywhere. I suspect *church hurt* drove Mom away from the church for most of her life, though she never told me.

Back in Mom's day, teen mothers were considered the worst of sinners. The church had a tendency to harshly judge teen moms, while the father moved onto the next unsuspecting female. I've heard stories about scared moms being dragged before the congregation to confess their sins as prying eyes bore into them with judgement. Both my mother and grandmother were teen mothers. Growing up in the south, I can only imagine how badly the church judged and treated them. Whatever the case, our spiritual lives were heavily impacted by religious practices and doctrine that was unfair.

We weren't in the pews, yet Mom made sure we understood the importance of having a relationship with God. I think this is the root of my present feelings about religion. I'm focused more on having a personal relationship with God than religious traditions and affiliations. Today, I'm a member of an amazing congregation, but that's secondary to my relationship with My Creator. Mom planted that in my soul. She taught us to respect God's moves over man's.

I remember not being able to watch television or move around the house during thunderstorms and sitting on the couch or laying down in our rooms to listen to the Master work. Mom explained that she learned the importance of respecting God during storms from her grandmother, whom she spent a lot of time with as a child. While at her house one evening, she was in the middle of making a sandwich when a storm came rushing in. "Come get in this bed until it passes!" her grandmother hollered. Mom didn't listen until lightening crashed through the kitchen window, striking the bread bag just as she was putting it on the counter. Mom didn't waste any time running and hiding under the covers in her grandmother's bed after that. She never *disrespected* the moves of God again. Her telling me the story was enough to keep me quiet when storms came.

Mom taught us to talk to God when we were in need and to thank Him for our blessings. She talked to God out loud which seemed strange until I found myself doing the same thing. Initially for me, God was crisis intervention. The one you call on when things aren't going as expected. He was like the distant relative we talk to on occasion - when they're out of sight, we don't think about them until something happens.

God was never far from Mom's mind. She made a practice of writing prayers and putting them in her Bible at Psalms 23. She told me whenever I have an urgent request to write it down and put it in the Bible, because God will always answer. Honestly, I blew off her advice. And after she died, it didn't seem like a way to elicit God's divine assistance. To me, asking anything was a betrayal.

My trust in God dwindled. Where there's no trust, there's no relationship. I never prayed much, but when I stopped trusting, I stopped praying. For the longest time, I barely acknowledged His existence. Why should I? My prayers weren't answered, so it was obvious He'd forgotten about me. That made it alright for me to forget Him, too. Grief is blinding. Causes us to forget the good and be content being miserable.

God healed my daughter. My anger at Him caused me to forget that. Several months after the funeral, I was still receiving insurance payouts, but I may as well been broke. Despite my poor eating habits, there was a healthy baby growing in my womb. But I could've been barren. Not even how quickly I secured my place in Norfolk made a difference. Maybe I would've been happier homeless. Most of all, God left my greatest prayer lingering in Heaven: He abandoned me.

None of these things I prayed out loud for. Didn't even know I desired them. I was praying in the Spirit. Yes, I wanted my children to be healthy and to have financial security, but I that didn't matter to me. I wanted everything I lost back. God denied my *one* request! So, I didn't want to talk to Him. Just like my father, he was absent. When I needed God most, He was ghost, and that's where I felt He should remain.

Anyone familiar with God knows that when destiny's waiting, His will be done, whether we agree with it or not. God is always available, but we must receive what He offers, because He'll never circumvent our free will. He wants us in a posture of surrender to receive all He has for us. True surrender reveals our vulnerability. Transparency reveals insecurities and illuminates open wounds. It's where healing occurs, and we find the strength to step into our destiny.

Most people believe that worship manifests through praise, hand claps, shouting, and external forms of gratitude to The Father. In its purest form, worship begins with surrender. When we trust God, we surrender to His will, rejecting preconceived notions about how our lives should be going. While He loves and cares for all His children in earnest, He selects a chosen few for His specific purpose and is relentless in His pursuit of us. Even though I broke up with Him, God did not break up with me. His reckless love for me caught me off guard. On my own, God knew I'd sever our relationship, so He used the one thing I craved most after losing Mom to draw me back to Him: *human relationships.*

The year before Mom died, Portsmouth rezoned the high schools, placing me at Mom's alma mater, I.C. Norcom High School. Due to a conflict with one of her teachers during senior year, Mom didn't graduate. Because she didn't finish, one of her greatest desires was for me to obtain my diploma. Walking into the alumni hall, it was gut-wrenching to see Mom's senior photo hanging on the wall. She was so close to achieving a dream that ended up so far out of reach. Transferring to I.C. Norcom gave me the opportunity to finish what Mom started.

As a student, I struck up a friendship with a girl I'll call Sheena. We got pretty close, but lost contact after graduation. Sheena graduated with the rest of the class in June. I graduated in August because I was unable to take Advanced placement English 11 while I was on homebound study and my fulfillment of the English requirement was delayed a semester. After that, I was too preoccupied with caring for my mother and daughter than striking up friendships with my peers.

I would visit Aunt Liv, who lived on the other side of the main road a lot. She was the only bright spot preventing me from self-destructing at the funeral. I missed Mom so much, I practically lived with Aunt Liv to reclaim a piece of her presence. During one of our frequent visits, I was walking home and ran into Sheena, who lived a block away. We started hanging out, which was a breath of fresh air. Sheena married in high school and started a family. I admired her so much for being the same age as me and having all the things I desperately wanted out of life. Especially a family to give and receive love.

Looking back, I can see how God used Sheena to draw me to Him. She was a Godly woman. Her discernment was unparalleled, and she wasn't afraid to show her faith. Once, Sheena was taking me apartment hunting when she abruptly stopped in the middle of our conversation to pray. She said she was finishing her fast; I didn't even know what fasting meant. She finished her prayer, then explained it to me. I appreciated her taking the time to help me instead of making me feel bad for not knowing.

Sheena had strong beliefs about ungodly behavior and didn't entertain anything contradicting her stance. If what she considered sin was involved, she had no problem correcting and urging folks to make positive changes. We had several conversations about sin that opened my mind to exploring more of God. I didn't agree with everything she said, I valued the relationship enough to not challenge her with my limited biblical knowledge and weak faith.

God has a wonderful sense of humor. Since I refused to talk to Him, He planted a young woman like me whom I trusted and genuinely liked in my path as a godly influence. The further away I pushed from Him, the harder He reeled me back in, using my friend as His mouthpiece. *Why haven't You given up on me, God? I left You a long time ago.*

Contrary to what I wanted, God had other plans.

I didn't get baptized when my nephew and brothers did, nor did I give my life to Christ. However, as my friendship with Sheena grew, my interest in God was piqued. So, I talked to her about what it meant to get saved and baptized. In turn, Sheena taught me about faith and salvation. I appreciated how she didn't mind being transparent and sharing God with me. Her excitement made me eager to go deeper in Him, and I listened intently as she taught.

One thing I really loved about Sheena is how direct she was. "You need to give your life to God," she told me. I was still angry with Him, but I listened to what Sheena was telling me. After all, nothing else I was doing was working. Anger wasn't working. Ignoring Him made me miserable. I didn't expect to just snap my fingers and be over Mom's death, but I'd hoped to process losing her more effectively. Sheena didn't beat me over the head with a Bible, shame, guilt or manipulate me into salvation. She captured me by showing me God's love. I was ready to come back to Him.

The day I gave my life to Christ, Sheena was by my side. I accompanied her when she traveled to visit her sister, who was on her own journey to Christ. "Do you want to live differently with Christ at the center of your life?" she asked as we gathered around her sister's dining room table.

"Yes we do," we said, almost in unison.

"Good," she said with a smile, "let's pray the prayer of salvation. Together."

I don't know what I thought was going to happen, but after we recited the prayer…nothing changed. Maybe I thought some miraculous, divine cloud would deliver me from the darkness that had been looming over me for so long, but it didn't. There were no fireworks, or sudden change in my attitude. There was, *nothing*.

But I came back to You, God.

That next Sunday, I was still unsure of myself. Something felt off. Mom was still dead, emptiness still in her place. In spite of how I felt, I pushed on and attended service with Sheena. Afterwards, she introduced me to her pastor, a tiny woman with great power. Pastor took me by the hands, her keen eyes boring through me. "You're confused about some things," she uttered in her authoritative voice. "Things that are causing you distress. Don't worry, everything will be alright. You're going to be just fine. God's going to give you clarity."

My cheeks burned scarlet. Did Pastor's prophecy have anything to do with the fact that I'd started questioning my sexuality? How could she know? Why would she call me out like that? I was so humiliated, I wanted to run out and never go back there again.

Why do you keep doing this to me, God?

It would take years for me to understand what Pastor was talking about. In that moment, I felt *seen*. Seen, and nervous. *I hope she can't tell just by looking. If she can, I'm in trouble.*

I'm by no means homophobic, but with everything I was already dealing with, I couldn't handle being a lesbian, too. Once I had time to think things through, I realized my curiosity was pretty common in many women. After giving it serious thought, I concluded that I loved men and not inclined to change my preference. Regardless, that prophecy stuck with me. God was giving me a glimpse of hope, proving He can be trusted. But just like with man, I needed God to earn my trust.

After getting saved, I found myself viewing everything concerning God through a magnifying glass. His influence over me, how He moved in my life. What most consider blessings, I scrutinized. It's the same way I am with my friends. I test my friends (and potential ones) with small things to see how they handle them. If they're genuine, my confidence in them grows, and I grant them greater access to my heart. See, I learned at an early age to be cautions of whom I call friend. I used that same practice in developing my relationship with God. The best friend of all.

I often wonder why I don't easily trust others. Scholars believe mistrust generally stems from neglect and emotional abuse during infancy. Parents who fail to build trust with their infants grow into adults who struggle in relationships - even their relationship with God. Because if we can't trust our earthly parents who are right here with us, how can we trust God who we can't see or hear?

God passed all of my tests. Believe me, I went all in! I was giving more of myself to Him, and needed to know He would come through for me. Mind you I was still grieving, but tired of being miserable and dwelling on the past. Problem was, I was so focused on living a godlier life, I wasn't honest about being in pain. I hadn't taken the time to heal my heart.

Those little things Mom did or said that made me love her so much randomly invaded my thoughts. Tears fell at unexpected times, but I stashed them away. Ignoring my plummeting emotional stability drove me into a serious bout of depression that lasted for several years. It didn't matter though, because I was getting back with God. Where I went wrong was stashing my feelings where I thought they'd be safe instead of giving it to God. I climbed into my shell, waiting for the darkness to come back and wreak havoc again. In the meantime, I focused on something else my life was missing; I wanted love.

Viewing Sheena's marriage from the outside, I wanted what she had - a husband, a father to help raise my children, a man with strong faith in God, and a lover who cherished me as a woman. I wanted a man I could trust and do life with. Sheena advised me to pray for the man I wanted. Just like Mom told me, Sheena said to write what I wanted and be specific about it.

I took Sheena's advice and went one step further. *"Don't forget to put it in the Bible baby,"* Mom's voice reminded me. So, I jotted down all the characteristics that I wanted in a mate, prayed, and slid my list in the Bible under Psalm 23, with hope and expectation in my heart.

CHAPTER 7

Cracks In The Clouds

Have you ever looked up in the sky after a storm? The sun peeking through the clouds, majestic shards of light forcing their way through the cracks in the sky, like they're commanding, *"Move out of the way, I need to shine!"* Pushing further between the clouds, the light brightens, drying the soggy earth. My prayer for a mate was written a month before I moved to Norfolk. Getting away felt like the light pushing through the stubborn clouds. I was still caught in unhealthy situation with Kesiara's biological father and wanted more for myself. I figured if God could help me find my *more*, I would give Him a shot.

Sometimes God shifts our lives to reposition us for purpose. Those shifts bring new seasons and challenges to overcome with them. Change causes fear because we tend to be too focused on what we're losing instead of opening our eyes to the fresh opportunities and blessings on the horizon. God wants to prepare us for new blessings; look at the challenges we encounter as training grounds to prepare us for greater.

Please understand that sometimes the shift includes people. Moving to Norfolk was my way of escaping to a new beginning. We like to believe the people we love most (*especially our parents*) are meant to be with us for a lifetime, so we place a lifetime of expectations on their shoulders. The problem is, we're making a mistake by putting that kind of pressure on people meant to for seasonal positions.

For the longest, I thought Mom was taken from me way too soon. In reality, according to the season, the timing was perfect. God placed Mom in my life for a season; her purpose was to birth and raise me to the age of maturation. Of course, I know I wasn't Mom's sole purpose; however, I was a crucial part of it. We're not always purposed to be *the one*. Our purpose may be to birth *The One*, like Mary did with Jesus. Now I'm not claiming to be Jesus, but God appointed me to help carry out Mom's destiny. No one else could carry out the assignment like I did because God purposed me for it.

I firmly believe that once we've served our purpose on earth, God calls us to our reward. It wasn't always perfect, but Mom diligently carried out her natural tasks. Once those were fulfilled, it was time for her to take her rest. Her death was the end that birthed a new beginning. The shift was finally making sense.

Moving to Norfolk in June of 1995 gave me more hope than I'd felt in forever. My trust was in God, but I was nervous about surrendering to His will. Still, I couldn't shake the feeling of His support. Now I didn't just hurl myself into the deep end without a life preserver, but I did something I hadn't done in a long time: I prayed hard before I moved.

Did I pray right? Is there even a right way to pray?

As weird as it felt, I was oddly optimistic. I started making decisions and doing things that contradicted who I was. Where I used to shrink, now I checked my family when they said things to offend me. I found my voice and would never be the same.

The bridge I was building between me and God was getting stronger, and my trust gained traction as I patiently waited for Him to send the life partner I prayed for. I didn't lose hope, but I expected a slower response to my prayer based on what I knew about God's timing. I didn't want to be alone. Someone to share my life with was my most pressing, unfulfilled desire. Adulting mandated that I raise my daughter, pay bills, manage my health, and take care of my new home. My financial situation was stable enough to put off getting a job for the time being, but I did want to work. A new set of plates piled on top of the ones that were already spinning. I prayed that I could manage them all.

The first day in my new apartment, God blew my mind with answered prayers. I lost so much, but it was amazing to find Him. After making everything else my idols, I was finally elevating Him to His rightful position in my life. The place my mother had previously occupied.

One of the scariest things I've done was refocusing on God. He helped me discover I wasn't as lonely as I thought I was. His absence was the void I needed to fill.

"I'll make this work whether You send me a partner or not," I promised God as I unpacked the new apartment. As bad as I wanted a man in my life, I patiently waited on God's timing, preparing my spirit for the blessing to manifest.

So, back to that first night in the apartment.

As blessings would have it, God's sense of humor showed up in the most hilarious way. The very day I moved in was the day I met the man who would change my life…Malcolm, my future husband. Right in my living room. Malcolm happened to be Jay's co-worker. I was over playing games with men, and wholeheartedly believed God would let me know when the right man came along. Thinking there was no way He works that fast, at first, I rejected Malcolm.

Is this really You, God?

I played it cool, engaging in a short, yet meaningful conversation with Malcolm that ended with me giving him my phone number. Up until that point, I had never given a man my number without him asking or struck up a conversation just to flirt before. And I was never as forward with anyone as I was with him. Comfortable, too. I don't know what came over me – I wasn't myself around him.

The shy, insecure me didn't feel worthy enough to give a man my number. That part of me was in the past. The more pressing question was, if it wasn't God, why was I drawn to Malcolm so quickly?

First of all, God was molding me. Once I surrendered control of my life to Him, I was far from the person I used to be. I did and said things that were totally out of character, but that's what surrendering to God means. Not just our thoughts, but our total selves. Even though I didn't know where things would lead, I trusted God with every part of me. My mind traveled back to the prophecy from Sheena's pastor. Everything was going to be alright.

Two days after Malcolm and I met, we began dating. After a week, we were living together. Anyone else would've been surprised at the relationship moving at such lightning speed, but I wasn't. Not even when we got engaged within four months and married a year and half from the day we met. That chance meeting in my living room shaped my future. So many things could've gone wrong (many things did), but it was all orchestrated by God. When we fell on rough times, neither of us gave up on our relationship. I'm grateful to say we're still thriving. God's plan continues to do that for us.

Throughout this entire process, God revealed His character and power. He showed me His infinite knowledge of my needs, wants and desires, and opened my eyes to the best interests for me, whether I liked them or not. For example, Mom was all about family over everything, and my family wasn't around. Still, I wanted to honor her wishes.

I got caught up in the *shoulds*—personal perceptions about what others do and how they should act. Like, "*My mother should love me because I'm her daughter,*" or "*You should help me because I helped you.*" Getting caught up in *should* thinking is a setup for disappointment, because not everyone shares our values. I felt like my family *should* want to be in my life, but God showed me He had more.

My relationship with Malcolm took away the loneliness, provided me with help in raising my daughters, and helped me to forge new relationships. It was a long time coming, but I had a community again. It wasn't the family I hoped for, but God created love ties to replace the blood ones He severed. Malcolm is from a large, close-knit family, and was raised in a working, middle-class neighborhood. A beautiful portrait of nuclear and extended families.

When we met, Malcolm's parents were living and still married, as well as his grandparents, several of his uncles, aunts, siblings, and cousins. Most importantly, they were friendly and didn't exhibit toxic traits like my family did. I'd never witnessed a family as close as they were. The fact that they accepted me as part of their tribe was overwhelming, especially with me being so much younger with a child on the way that wasn't his. To them, those things didn't matter. They considered my heart, which was exactly what I needed.

I met Malcolm's mother a month after we started dating. The plan was to meet her prior to our date to a Chris Tucker comedy show, and I was super nervous. But as soon as I arrived at her house, I realized there was no need for me to be nervous. She was so warm, welcoming me with motherly eyes.

"Malcolm told me that your mother passed recently," she said.

"Yes ma'am, she did." I nearly choked on the confirmation, but I spit it out the best I could.

"Well, I'm your mother now. If you need anything, you just let me know. Call me Mama Lucy."

Oddly enough, hearing those words gave me the assurance things would truly be different going forward.

Some may think I should've been offended. How dare a woman who was a practical stranger offer to replace my mother! My *everything*. But I didn't see it that way. As a black woman raised in a black community, the idea of having several *mothers* – a village, isn't foreign to me. Though there is only one biological mother, having a bonus mother, a *big mama*, or *Mama [insert a name]* is the norm in the Black community. These were the women who raised and nurtured the village. The seasoned elders who stepped in to provide guidance, protection, and love regardless of the where the biological mother was. Mama Lucy was offering to be my village.

Mama Lucy provided so much that I was missing when I lost Mom. Comfort, a sense of belonging, assurance that someone cared about me, and love. She was my second mother until her transition 15 years later. Her selfless love taught me that love-ties can be more significant than blood ones. God used her to instill that in me.

Unconsciously, I began understanding that meticulously outlining my life wouldn't reveal what I needed; I simply needed to follow God's lead. From the date I surrendered to Him, I strived to make good decisions. Don't get me wrong - I messed up a lot along the way, but I fought to get back on track, even without knowing what was ahead.

CHAPTER 8

Action Steps

For years, I felt like I was living in the dark. Confined to a room with very little light to see. In the dark, things get in my way and I bump into them. It doesn't kill me or stop my progression. I see them as additional obstacles to climb.

I'm not in the room alone. There's someone guiding, teaching, warning of danger ahead, and chastising my bad behavior, loss of motivation, and self-sabotage. I can't see what's on the sides of me because I have blinders on. I can only see when I'm doing well, everything else is irrelevant.

Then there are those times when I'm running blind, afraid to make a fool of myself. The voice in the room always provides direction. At times I trust it, others I don't. However, it persists. The tears fade, but the grief's still there. Replaced by focus, determination, and drive. God and I are still building, challenges arise. But I keep moving. I don't always understand, but I keep on moving.

From age 19 to 35, I tried obeying the direction of God. Trusting Him was hard but, I made a commitment to see the tough times through. Now I say it was hard because of the challenges I faced. Was it really God? I mean, I thought life would get better once I completely gave myself over to Him, but things seemed to be getting worse. Especially my relationship with Malcolm. Our conflicts eclipsed the good things that were happing for us.

Our problems started well before jumping the broom. Simply put, our exes gave us hell. His ex-wife and her heavy-handed opinions on how he should parent their two children. My ex-boyfriend with his skewed version of the truth and inconsistencies. It was exhausting. The issues in our blended family went on until our children grew up. Far too long. I'd say we were happy for about four years before letting down our guards, which opened a whole new world of drama. I wanted more attention, Malcolm wanted peace. Peace from arguing over bills, kids, and money.

I hammered Malcolm about working multiple jobs keeping him away from home; he dragged me for not being a better homemaker. I won't lie - I sucked at cleaning. Still do. He also wanted me to be more independent. "What if something happens to me," he fussed, "you can't take care of everyone or yourself without a job." I was angry that he brought up the fact that I never got a job after my second daughter was born, but he was right. But as expensive as daycare was, I was better off taking care of the kids myself at home.

Did I mention Malcolm and I had two more children together? Yes…our blended family of six had blossomed to eight. By the time I was 22, I had birthed four children. The mounting tension caused us to be easily influenced by people who had no business in our marriage. Things turned so dreadful between Malcolm and me, I thought God had been lying to me for the last eight years. And I slipped right back into darkness.

We were on the brink of divorce. When we weren't bumping heads, there was little to no communication at all. Neither Malcolm nor I cared about each other's needs. Thankfully, God made us stop, focus, and regroup before we gave up. Some people call it instinct or intuition, others call it karma or fate. Some folks even refer to it as discernment or the ancestors speaking. I call it the *Holy Spirit*.

The Holy Spirit provokes us to do what's right. How do we know the Holy Spirit is speaking? Because She'll never encourage us to commit wrongdoing or engage in sin. She will challenge and make us uncomfortable; whatever She asks requires sacrifice, work and laser focus. When God tells us a thing, we must adapt to His way of thinking. In other words, the Holy Spirit invites us to consider what God would want us to do. Our task is to discern what the Spirit is saying. Proper discernment takes practice, prayer, faith, and trust in The One who influences us internally.

In Malcolm's and my eyes, our marriage was over. We saw each other as emotionally abusive, and were too weary to work things out, individually or together. Thank God the Holy Spirit intervened and opened our eyes to how fractured our relationship truly was. We realized both of us wanted *more*. Not just *from* each other, but *for* each other. We had to pivot and commit to prioritizing one another, our relationship, needs and desires. The children were never an issue; we were crappy mates, but our kids were well taken care of. We pushed selfishness aside and refocused on restoring our relationship and saving our family.

In the meantime, Malcolm was restless at work and I couldn't blame him. The physical strain was beating him down. It was hard looking into his eyes every day, being stuck in a job that wasn't good for him, knowing he was longing for a better life.

"Why don't you go back to college?" I suggested. "Finish the degree you started."

"I've got you and the kids. I don't know if I can do it," he countered.

I stared him directly in the eyes to prove I had confidence in him. "How will you know unless you try? You won't have to do this alone."

Despite uncertainty, Malcolm re-enrolled in school. Pursuing his degree piled a ton of added responsibility on his plate, so I stepped up and showed my support by helping with his studies. It wasn't easy, but our team of two took him all the way from an associate degree to master's. Helping him made me feel like I was in school too; watching him walk across the stage to accept his MBA made the long nights well worth it. And when he secured a job as a manager at a local surgical center, I couldn't have been prouder. Watching Malcolm grow and better himself was incredible! My process; however, was a bit more complicated.

Our youngest daughter was starting pre-school, when I heard the Holy Spirit say, "What will you do when your children are grown and your husband is out living his life?"

I was struck to my core, suddenly self-conscious and unfulfilled. A vision of myself as an old woman wasting away at home while my husband and children, successful and off living their best lives surrounded by people who loved them frightened me to death. *What do I want from life?* I thought. And what did God want from me? I was just as smart as Malcolm – helping him get through school proved that. I could conquer college, too. No one in my family had gone on to continuing education, why not start with me?

Immediately, I enrolled in community college. The first day of classed I was so excited, I almost forgot to get dressed before racing down to the school. Once I got there, I wished I had slowed down. I was so unhappy. College was nothing like what I'd seen depicted on the television show *A Different World*. College life on that show was so fun and lively, filled with people who looked like me, working towards fulfilling their dreams. At least they knew what they wanted; I didn't have a clue what my dreams were. Before I had the chance to give up on myself and education, God interceded on my behalf once again.

I enrolled at Norfolk State University after completing a year and a half of community college. Initially, I intended to go to school to become a teacher, but after volunteering at my kids' elementary school, I realized teaching wasn't for me. Putting up with a thankless job, dealing with insufferable parents wasn't my passion, nor did I have the patience. So, I started my next phase of school without declaring a major. Whatever it was, it wouldn't have a thing to do with education.

On orientation day, while other freshmen had their parents helping them make decisions about their majors and what classes to enroll in, Malcolm was helping me. Thankfully, I stumbled across the university's Director of the Bachelor of Social Work program, who provided me with some much-needed guidance. As she explained what it would take to obtain a degree in social work and its benefits, my spirit whispered, "*This is it*," confirming I was where I belonged. From that day forward, I pursued a master's degree in social work, with an emphasis on mental health. Following graduation, after years of talking about it, I finally got a job: a therapist at an acute care mental health hospital. I was a working woman!

Despite all these blessings, I was still trapped in darkness, waiting on snatches of light to shine. College, work, improved relationships, being close to some of my family. It all weighed heavily on me. I was unable to connect my achievements to purpose. At least God was allowing me to prove my doubters wrong, increase my self-esteem, and be a positive example for my children. My voice was getting louder; influence greater. I was even making friends and gaining work experience that would eventually help me earn my license to practice social work. Still, as my professional life was coming together, my spirit experienced another shift.

Oddly enough, the next shift began at a funeral. Almost every major shift in my life has been shrouded in death. My mentor's mother died. Her brother (a bishop at a megachurch in Maryland), delivered an eloquent eulogy, packed with emotion, power, and strength. Listening to his passionate sentiments, the Holy Spirit spoke to me:

"That's going to be you."

Such a small declaration may have gone unnoticed by anyone else, but it momentarily paralyzed me. I silently acted as though I hadn't heard what the Spirit said. Then I convinced myself the voice meant I was destined to be a public speaker, destined to educate the masses on the importance of mental health. I wasn't wrong…I just wasn't completely right.

When challenged, I hear what I want to hear, so I can stay in my comfort zone. That's why I ignored what I knew was *The Call*. God and I had grown so much closer. I'd gotten baptized and joined my husband's family's church, but things were getting tense there and I was contemplating leaving. Certainly, God wasn't calling me in the middle of all this mess. I didn't want to be a minister, anyway. Not until everything was straightened out. So, for the next eight years, I ran from my calling.

I'd already been on the run from God six years before I started butting heads with my pastor. I was a ministry leader, but it I wasn't happy at that church. I could've gone to Pastor to explain how I wanted to get my ministry license, which would've taken three months. I chose not to, because something didn't feel right. I couldn't stand him – why have him license me? Then there was the congregation, who rejected and didn't support me in ministry. I remember spending an entire month promoting a women's group where ladies of the church could come together to discuss all things female. Outside of my cousin who was the co-facilitator, not one woman was interested. And no one showed up at the interest meeting. I was devastated.

Neither the pastor nor his wife stood by me. I was allowed to speak during service, but my messages were widely ignored. Not that I believe it was done maliciously, but I do believe it was God. For two years, He'd been telling me to leave that church; however, I refused to take heed, because that's where Malcolm grew up. Staying there out of disobedience made life miserable. Stepping into the sanctuary sparked an uncontrollable rage in me; who gets angry over going to church? Unless the church is hurting instead of healing.

I sat in the pews, raw emotions balled into fists, pummeling me as I tried pretending that I was okay. Everything and everyone seemed to swing at me, including the sermons. Was Pastor preaching on me? Things didn't improve after the benediction, either. In fact, when church was over, I felt worse. Eventually, I quit attending regularly, wasn't tithing, and stopped viewing the church as a place of healing. I was spiritually depleted. Walking in that church one more time was going to kill me.

"We have to get out of there," I finally told Malcolm when the dam was about to break. He didn't make me feel guilty that he'd be leaving the spiritual home he'd grown up in. Didn't berate, chastise or accuse me of being selfish. Didn't try to talk me out of it. Malcolm simply replied, "Okay."

Shortly after we made the decision to leave, we found an amazing church. I didn't have to worry about being a leader or taking on responsibilities I wasn't prepared for. All I had to do was sit in the pew and receive the Word. The relationships that would solidify my future there would come later, I was sure of that. Until then, I had to make it through another shift.

Now you know I struggle with shifting, so doing it again brought my nerves to an all-time high. God's sense of humor showed up once again, when He told me it was time to pursue a Master's in Divinity. I heard Him clearly, but because I was uncomfortable, I played like I hadn't. Again.

No, God! Wasn't putting myself through school and helping my husband enough?

I didn't want to go back. Papers, group projects, student loan debt. No! I decided to help God out by doing what I wanted to do - apply to the *Ministers in Training* program. Why did I even pull a stunt like that, knowing it wasn't what God said to do? Of course, I was denied admission to the program because I was going against God's will. It was so funny, I couldn't even be upset. There was only one person who was responsible for me not getting in: ME.

You know what you have to do.

One morning as I showered, I recited my goals out loud. "I'm going to study for my social work license, pass the exam with flying colors, get my Master's in Divinity, then…"

Wait, what? Who said that?

Hold up – that wasn't part of the plan. How did I even let that slip out of my mouth? How was I thinking pursuing a PhD in social work, but speaking Master's in Divinity?

"Okay, God. You win," I sighed. "I'll apply, but since this is Your will, this is Your bill. I need You to pay for my education because I don't have any money."

I applied and was swiftly admitted without any problems.

This was the time to celebrate, right? Not necessarily balloons, music and cake, but at least some alone time to bask in the glow of my latest accomplishment. And it would've been, had it not been for the darkness creeping right back in. This was another piece of the puzzle coming together. The problem was, there was a picture coming together, but I didn't have a reference point to tell me if it was the right one.

Am I doing the right thing?

For 16 years, I did my best not to bump into the walls in the darkness. God and the Holy Spirit were guiding and keeping me from wrecking my life. Relationships were elevated or halted, blessed opportunities were revealed and those meant to burn me were exposed. Rejections persisted and blessings overflowed. All the while, I kept moving without an understanding, plan, or knowing what I was getting into. That's faith, honey!

Along the way, I dealt with more unexpected deaths and disappointments, tempered with joy, love, and peace. But what do you do when your faith starts fizzling out, and you're left with more questions than answers? When the cracks start showing up in your armor, will you finally be ready to tackle the grief you've been running from?

CHAPTER 9

Finding Focus

With no clear plan, direction, or divine instructions, I lost my motivation. I was disinterested in everything, until I was reminded of a story that my mom shared during one of our talks.

My maternal grandmother died of tuberculosis when Mom was 16 and pregnant. After living with her father for a short period of time, Mom settled in Virginia with her grandfather.

"How did you deal with her dying?" I wondered aloud.

"It wasn't easy," she replied, "but I got through it."

At the time, she was a young, single parent who was afraid. Then she told me something that was all too familiar: She was also severely depressed. She retreated to her room, isolated away from everyone, barely eating or functioning. Severely withdrawn and hopeless, Mom spent her days staring at the ceiling, flooded with tears. After weeks of wallowing in sorrow, Mom's grandfather came into her room and gently admonished, "Annette, your mother is dead, you are not." No wonder she loved him so much. His words were harsh, but he delivered them in love. And it was just what she needed to refocus and pull herself together.

I'd become my mother.

What I needed was focus, drive, and inspiration to conquer my swelling list of responsibilities. Walking to a destination without a map had worn me out. Something needed to spark my enthusiasm, I just didn't know what that something was. Somehow, I managed to be at peace with not knowing.

"God, what's the end goal here?" I prayed. "Where's all of this leading? How long is it going to take to reach the goals You set for me? What am I doing?"

I wanted to rush the process and skip over the *unnecessary* experiences, *useless* lessons, and endless heartbreak that plagued my life for so long and get to the good part! Greatness is within me; I've known that for a long time. I just didn't understand that greatness comes with a price. A price I wasn't sure I could afford. If I'd been billed for all the valleys that brought me to purpose, I'd be in debt forever.

One thing I was lacking to help others was a reference point to draw from. Theoretically, we can claim to understand someone's pain; however, in order to help them through it we need first-hand knowledge of turmoil's aftermath and the recovery that comes with it. My experiences – both good and bad, taught me how to use my life as an example to help others understand the present isn't the end, but a part of the process. I tried to skip over the pain, pleading for God to set me free. I cried out to Him so much, my pleas were akin to breathing. And when I didn't hear God respond, I missed the fact that He was directing me exactly where I needed to go.

On the surface, life was exciting. I settled in my career, was a member of an awesome church, and my family was thriving. But mediocrity got me stuck and stagnant. There was a ton of work to get done that I was too tired to do. I had to though, or I'd disappoint God, the same as Mom. Quitting wasn't an option…I had to find the motivation somewhere.

Motivation meant training my brain to see the inspiration in the small things. Setting realistic goals kept me moving and focused. I wasn't privy to the complete vision God had for me; however, I was stepping towards destiny. That's what kept me going back then, and now when life gets tough. The only failure for me is stopping.

I met my best friend, Christopher, in college. Outside of my husband, he knows me best. Over the years, our relationship has grown from friendship to family. Now when we met, I didn't particularly care for him. He came across as arrogant, and I couldn't stand him. His tremendous heart wasn't visible, but I hung in there until I got to see it. It took a lot of getting to know each other and open communication for me to figure out that part.

They're Gone! Now What?

Many college students find it easier to drop out than deal with demanding professors, deadlines, and peers while juggling work, home, and faith. That's where Christopher and I encouraged one another to see it through. We found ourselves with undergraduate degrees, prepped to enter graduate school in *advanced standing* together (advanced standing is a graduate program that consists of a year and a half of vigorous educational training rather than the normal graduate school track). At the last minute, I withdrew my application, choosing to traditionally complete my studies at our alma mater, while my friend enrolled in another university 75 miles away.

The last semester of his graduate year, he called me. When I answered his call, I wasn't expecting to hear, "It's too hard. I'm done."

"You're not talking about quitting, are you?" I quietly waited for him to confirm; he answered me with silence.

"I've got all these papers, the internship takes up most of my time, and my professors don't believe I can do it," he stammered. "Maybe they're right. It's best for me to walk away."

Patience has never been a gift of mine, but I held on, listening to him vent, doing all he could to get a co-sign from me. He wasn't going to get it.

"Stop tripping," I fussed after giving him enough time to spit his feelings out. "We don't have time for this. You're staying right where you are, and you're going to finish. Both of us are. Call me when you get out of class…you got this."

Tough love from me was what my friend needed. However, I didn't know how my own advice would come roaring back on me.

A year later, I was preparing for graduation. Once again, flailing in the deep end of the pool. I'd lost both my in-laws, my daughters were going through their *terrible teens*, our finances were pitiful and on top of everything else, I had three massive papers due that were still blank pages. Disgusted and completely stressed out, I snatched the phone, dialed my best friend's number, and told him I was quitting…

…and he threw everything I'd thrown at him a year earlier right back at me.

Because he loved me.

After I walked across the stage and held the satisfaction of the master's degree I'd worked so hard to earn in my hands, it was like the pain subsiding after giving birth. My friend and I laugh about the situation now, but while we were in the midst of giving up, things had gotten pretty serious. As tough as it was, finishing school taught me how to set my destructive thoughts aside, focus on my goals complete the task, no matter how I felt. Feelings can betray us when we let them sneak up; we have to finish what we start, regardless.

Since graduation, I've often implemented this strategy in the vast majority of my life, especially in my relationship with God. He has strategically planted me in seasons that seem crazy, yet I've kept moving forward, even when I didn't believe that I could. But if God has faith that I'll succeed, then I'll keep right on pushing. This perspective takes the pressure off me so I can focus on those things I can control, and let God handle the rest.

Conquering mental strain means finding the reason WHY. Why is it so important? Why is it crucial not to quit? Why even try? Having someone or something to keep us balanced helps alleviate anxiety of the unknown. Connecting to our inspiration simultaneously connects us with our purpose. It opens our limited world view and ignites us to explore new possibilities. Most importantly, it'll change the way we see ourselves. Suddenly, defeat becomes victory, or apathy transforms to determination. Inspiration becomes the birthing room where stagnation was once the morgue.

To live, breathe, and move forward, we need to find what gives us life. For me, it was my husband and children. My children are my jewels; every time they shine their light on me, I am simply inspired! Them watching me drives me to succeed. If I can help it, my kids won't ever see their mother as a woman who settled, when she could have exceeded beyond any stretch of the imagination. I want my wins to fuel my children with the strength to pursue their dreams. When they look at me, I want them to see *HOPE*. So, no – I can't quit. There're tons of adorable pictures of my jewels on my phone to keep me from giving up when the urge hits or things get too hard. I look at them and know without a doubt, they are my reason *WHY*.

Malcolm inspires me for entirely different reasons. Every aspect of his life speaks of his determination to succeed. From being born with cerebral palsy, struggling to navigate the world outside the womb, to relying on braces to walk and later functioning on his own, Malcolm's always been a fighter.

For instance, at five-years-old, Malcolm saw his classmates racing around the room, playing without braces like him. Frustrated - but without pouting or crying, Malcolm plopped in the middle of the floor, snatched the braces off, and refused to put them back on. He was going to play with the other kids and wouldn't be denied! His teacher called home, explaining that since Malcolm refused to wear the protective gear and was running around in socks, his mother needed to get down to the school with some shoes as soon as she could. From then on, Malcolm never wore braces again. He literally took a stand, and never turned back.

From the time he was born, Malcolm's life has been filled with physical and emotional challenges, but he's never allowed others to place limitations on him, and he's never quit on himself. Even the countless surgeries leading up to his 15th birthday failed to slow him down. He accepted his uniqueness, pushing through with power. He used that power to convince his mother to abandon plans for more surgeries to correct his gait, feet, and ankles. Malcolm was happy to be who God created him to be and wanted to be free. She was hurt, but Mama Lucy consented to let the surgeries go. And Malcolm's become a better version of himself for it.

Whenever I want to give up, I think about that little boy, who desired to run with everyone else. He inspires me to run, too. The way he conquered challenges others saw as impossible, compels me to keep moving. His hope gives me hope; I don't have to focus on the destination, I just run.

The other person I look to for inspiration stares at me from the mirror. There was time I worked for an acute care mental health facility, facilitating therapy group sessions. One of the group exercises was to read the poem, *The Man in the Glass*, a poem of self-perception, by Peter Dale Wimbrow, Sr. Wimbrow writes that what we think of ourselves far outweighs what others think of us. It's in the vein that I instructed the patients that once they returned to their rooms, to look in the mirror and assess what they saw. Then, they were to stare that person in the eye and talk to them. Because the eyes never lie. *"Don't be afraid. Just be real with yourself about who you see looking back at you,"* I advised them.

On the surface, truth, trauma, low self-esteem, shame, guilt, and overwhelming sadness jumped out from their reflections; however, I encouraged them to look deeper for strength, hope, and life. As long as we're breathing, life is there…sometimes we just need to look deeper.

The eyes are where we can also discover hope. There's this picture of me at four years old, sitting in an instant photo booth on my aunt's lap with a scowl plastered to my face. Not even a bucket of candy could force me to smile that day, though maybe she should have tried. The crazy thing is, all of my childhood photos look the same way. *Downtrodden.* You can sift through tons of photos and won't spot a single smile. I often wonder why? I don't remember being excessively sad or anything, but I also don't remember much about those days. Was I just a pensive child? Who knows?

As an adult, I want the peace that appeared to be missing from that little girl's world. I want her to smile proudly and know she's going to be okay. That *we're* going to be okay. When I'm overwhelmed and want to give up, I can look in her eyes, and find the strength to keep moving. I want her to be delighted with me and know that everything we've been through has purpose. I want to encourage the younger me to lead to a successful life.

My group strategies have worked wonders for me, too – they're permanent fixtures in my life. They helped me see I have too much riding on successfully completing God's plan for my life. However, pain can only be ignored for so long. I was so busy grinding on my professional and spiritual goals, that I ignored the cracks that began sprouting through my armor. The wound of losing my mother reopened again, causing me to lose my footing. I watched in horror as the invisible plates crashed around me. While I struggled to steady the remaining plates in one hand, I desperately clung to a sharp self-admission in the other: It was time to find new anchors for my peace, and deal with that pain that had been festering for 21 years.

CHAPTER 10

New Anchors

My life was overloaded. I didn't have wise counsel to help me hold onto the rope before I reached the end of it. The voids left by my Mom's and my mother-in-law's passing grew wider; with them gone I was at an impasse.

Don't get me wrong, Malcolm has always been there to give me advice. However, the kind of wisdom I need isn't exactly his forte. He's a fixer. Tell him the problem, and he'll move Heaven and earth to find a solution. Family's priority to my husband, and he does whatever he needs to make things right. My issues were beyond his abilities, especially helping me through severe depression. Insomnia, agitation, more *blah* days than good ones. All the classic symptoms snaked away my motivation and energy. And I hid it well.

At work, Chris (we were both therapists at this point) recognized the changes in me; my extended family was clueless. I guess I really had become an expert at thriving behind the mask. Except, I began lashing out at Malcolm. Out of nowhere, I'd yell and bring drama he didn't ask for. Until he had enough and confronted me about my erratic behavior.

"You're depressed and you're taking it out on me," he casually informed me one day. After running down the list of signs that up until that point I'd ignored, Malcolm warned me, "Get some help, or it's going to be me and you." He was kidding...but the truth was laced throughout the humor.

He's got some nerve, I thought. *I'm a therapist at a psychiatric hospital, and I'm familiar with all the signs of depression. I'm not even suicidal.*

The frustration I felt daily wasn't anything I couldn't handle on my own. The problem with emotional independence is that our gifts aren't for us, they're for others. Our view is too distorted to treat ourselves; close proximity to the situation leads to bad decisions. It's our responsibility to get help from someone else, even if it's a professional. Knowing this, I told Malcolm I'd think about therapy, fully intending to brush him off. The next day at work, I told Chris about our conversation. "Malcolm's right," he confirmed. "We have deep conversations about what's going on with you. It's time for you to pay someone who can help you." After that, I got over myself and my self-diagnosing, and found a counselor right away. Isn't it funny how we don't pay attention to our mate's advice until someone else says it?

After entering therapy, things got worse before they got better. Therapy is HARD. Once one layer is peeled back, a thousand other issues surface. We convince ourselves certain situations won't or don't impact us; however, once they're uncovered, we're overwhelmed.

When I started therapy, the lack of relationship with my father took precedence in our discussions. Processing my feelings towards him was like vomit extracting from my body. Dealing with him forced me to confront all of my parental issues. Some weeks, I was able to freely convey my feelings and heal from my pain. Other times, I was too depressed to open up. After so much back and forth, my therapist threatened to prescribe medication if I wasn't able to pull myself together.

Make no mistake, there is nothing wrong with pharmacotherapy. In many situations it's necessary when coping skills, effective communication, and a strong support system (therapists, peers, family) are ineffective. However, I didn't want to be prescribed anti-depressants. I wanted the opportunity to implement the coping skills I'd learned without relying on drugs. Besides, I was already taking medication for other health issues and didn't want more. So, I put in the work and *got my mind right.*

The past six years in therapy have been so powerful for me. Not only have I been able to work through my issues with my parents, but I've dealt with my tumultuous childhood, family rejection, and have even improved my relationship with God. My therapist is a chaplain whose own relationship with God gives her a unique perspective on various subjects including faith, business, and healing.

I've learned so much about myself, healed, stabilized my depression, gotten anxiety under control, and gained perspective on my spiritual calling. I've also learned the benefits of accepting our feelings, the power of forgiveness, and the strength of understanding our *why*. Oddly enough, these are also the most difficult realities I've had to face.

Therapy taught me because I was so busy hiding from the world behind my happy visage, I disconnected from my true feelings. I believed my own lies, which didn't make sense because I was crying all the time. Pretending was tiresome. Removing the mask and getting real helped me create a safe space to be myself and unload years of pent-up emotions. Finally, I could vent about my father, my family…God. Yes, I was still angry with Him. And the pain of losing both mothers in my life along with a string of other close family and friends stung like crazy. Sheena was one of the loved ones I lost.

Sheena died from bone cancer. Ironically, the friend whose life had brought me so close to God, drove me away from Him in death. Sheena dying was the final straw; I was mad at God again. Furious, even. But until therapy, I was afraid to admit that out loud. So many questions hovered over me until therapy unlocked the answers. That's where I found my voice, and I turned up the volume.

Someone may read this and think it is sinful to be angry with God. However, real people who have experienced Him know that it's alright to be upset when

He doesn't move the way we expect. A person who is mature in faith understands that God can handle anything, including our anger. Anger doesn't mean we don't love Him or value His relationship, it's simply a safe place for us to be authentic. He is our safe place.

Therapy doesn't work unless we're transparent. Starting with ourselves. First, I had to admit I suffered from survivor's guilt. I literally felt bad for outliving my mother. "*I want to die first*," I told Mom for the longest time. Life without her is something I never imagined or wanted to experience. Not my mother. Now that she's gone, it seemed wrong to breathe the air that she couldn't. I put that energy into pressuring myself to be the best at everything, which triggered anxiety, making it even more difficult to overcome my other issues.

I just want to make her proud, I'd say to justify being so hard on myself. Truth is, I wanted to prove living wasn't a mistake. That I didn't need to die to make things right. What was wrong? Being as successful as I am. Becoming a therapist, a great mother and wife; being called by God for greatness. But I am *all* those things. And I'm going to be an outstanding author and minister, too. I couldn't voice these affirmations before, but now I have no problem telling anyone within earshot how blessed and gifted I am!

Next, it was time to face another source of guilt: Loving my mother-in-law as much as I loved Mom. Not a day went by that I didn't dream of Malcolm's mother every time I closed my eyes. In the absence of Mom, I was attached to Mama Lucy, which caused me to feel guilt when thoughts of Mom were replaced with her. I found myself forcing Mom back into my mind to keep from feeling like I was dishonoring her memory. At one time, I thought maybe I loved Mama Lucy more than I loved Mom. As irrational as it was, I finally accepted the fact that I didn't have to choose between the two women I loved. After all, they were both my mothers: one birthed me, the other nurtured me. And I was okay with that.

Now, it was time to accept all of me. Sometimes, accepting myself as a therapist was easier than accepting that I'm chosen by God to have a powerful ministry. I had years to prepare for social work…who prepared me to teach *The Word*? Because of my training, I can efficiently and effortlessly provide therapy in my sleep. My peers respect me, and while I don't know everything, I know what I know. I wished I was that comfortable in ministry.

Once, I attended a business class at church, and the facilitator admonished us not to be afraid to be in the company of giants, like Caleb and Joshua in the Bible, who weren't afraid of the giants who believed they could take over Canaan. My problem was the giants had me afraid to fully walk in my purpose as a minister—one of the reasons I rejected my call for so long. It took some time, but through therapy, prayer, and believing that God doesn't make mistakes, I had faith to believe I was capable of *The Call*. I didn't have to reject ministry, and in order to minister I didn't have to turn my back on business. Both sides of me deserved to live. And because I honor ministry and business, I'm a force to be reckoned with!

Finding forgiveness was possibly the hardest lesson I learned throughout this process. I was angry with myself, my family, God…even Mom. All the wrongs I thought had been done to me had me furious, especially Mom's *decision* to die. I was so mad at her for yielding to my consent and dying, and equally upset with God for taking her away. Of course, my logic was faulty, but that's what happens when emotions aren't properly addressed. The anger festering inside me needed to go before it killed me.

Forgiveness is for the person who gifts it, not the one who committed the offense. As a therapist, what troubles me most is seeing patients harboring anger towards people who either don't even know it or are already dead. "Why do you allow others to have so much control over your life?" I ask them. "Those people are either living their best lives or have moved on to their reward." Then I question why they allow unforgiveness to erode their psyche and harden their hearts. Usually, there's not a solid answer. But at least I get them to thinking.

I learned to let go and forgive. I'd like to say there is a simple process to forgiving; truth is, there's not a recipe. It took talking out my feelings, listening to my therapist, challenging my negative thoughts, and officially releasing my anger, but I did it! Anger is a comfortable place; the easiest for unforgiveness to fester. However, by releasing the resentment of many years, I unleashed my authentic self. One who isn't bound by bitterness, and in control of my destiny. The woman God always intended me to be, that I ran so hard to escape. The minister who freed herself from self-imposed limitations and setbacks. The woman I could face in the mirror.

Breaking through wasn't an easy, nor quick process. There were times I felt I'd forgiven, but something I suddenly remembered made me angry all over again. Then I'd have to restart from the beginning. Forgiveness gave me the courage to accept the why's behind my anger. Why did I go through those things, and why had I lost so many people I loved? Most importantly, why had destiny put me through so much when I still didn't know the destination?

There are many why's for the things we experience. The why's remind me the challenges I've faced weren't for nothing or by coincidence. God used therapy to reveal many of my why's. Why did Mom die when she did? So that I could move towards my destiny, and help others deal with the grief of losing a loved one. For instance, I didn't realize how making arrangements for Mom's funeral helped me be there for Malcolm and his siblings as they planned Mama Lucy's 16 years later.

The last things Malcolm and his family wanted to concern themselves with after Mama Lucy died were things like insurance policy particulars for funeral cost coverage, who to contact after she transitioned, what flowers to purchase, and all the other minute details that tend to get lost in the shuffle. Since I'd already been through it, I was able to offer tangible help beyond sharing tears and comforting words. I got things done. Had I not navigated the grief process myself, I wouldn't be able to help others who are struggling with losing relationships, opportunities, or dealing with death. Surviving loss has helped me become a credible source of support from first-hand experience. Although it hurts while we go through it, knowing purpose is waiting on the other side of pain makes it all worth it.

The other important *why* for me was separating from my family and isolating from most everyone else. A few people I cared about remained in my life, like Christopher, Jay (who moved to Norfolk with me) and Malcolm's family; however, most of the people I grew up with and went to school with disappeared. It's easy to reminisce and get caught up in generalizations, such as, *I didn't have any family or any friends*, when reality doesn't exactly match up. It's important to be factual when processing our *why*. Be careful not to clump every person or event into a single category, where they don't belong.

I've always wanted friends but as I've gotten older - even while in college, I haven't been able to increase the number of people in my circle. Sure, I've made friends, but for any number of reasons, after a while they've fallen back. Losing contact with them for no apparent reason has been perplexing, but I move on. Separating from my blood family; however, has been easier. No one should be subjected to abuse and expected to take it just because the aggressor is *family*. I've never fit in with my family, like being rejected from a clique. Do they love me? Probably. But not like they love each other. And it hurts. Bad. Because all I've ever wanted is their love and acceptance.

I always wondered why I wasn't able to cultivate many long-lasting relationships.

"*Why is it so important to you?*" God asked me one day.

My response was, "Do You really exist?"

How could I question God that way? I was desperate for a connection. I had my husband, best friend, children, and people I loved, but when I saw others enjoying life with a load of friends, going to parties and other functions, having a blast, I wanted fun, too. I realized I wanted to be surrounded by that kind of love. Why was I the only one who was undeserving of it?

Why, God?

One morning, I lay in bed awake with my eyes closed. Home alone, mind clear. God answered my question with, "*I am here.*"

To me, God's voice sounded like a middle-aged, soft-spoken man. In hindsight I know that sounds weird, but I think He wanted to really get my attention and didn't want me to confuse His voice with something or someone else. I knew the voice belonged to Him without doubt. My eyes flew open, and I was instantly filled with clarity. God was who I needed; He set me apart. I didn't need to fit in. Everything that is unique to me (thoughts, experiences, views) are strategically designed by God for His purpose. All He asks is that I be patient with not knowing the *why's* behind His moves yet understand that my obedience is still required. As His child, I am obligated to give Him my best and follow His guidance. Hearing Him so clearly helped me take heed to Him without struggle, and accept who I am, as well as how I came to be.

I finally accepted me.

CHAPTER 11

Now What?

The night Mom died, I went to a neighbor's house instead of going home. She picked me up from the hospital, knowing I didn't want to be alone. As we climbed her porch steps to go into the house, I looked up at the sky and saw beautiful clouds. They were breathtaking; so striking, they seemed to command attention. The soft billowing rows of white cotton were like nothing I've ever seen before or since. They seemed so close, almost as if we could reach up and touch them. They brought me so much peace, I exhaled and soaked them in. Maybe God was sending me a sign that Mom was safe, and I would be fine. That's what I chose to believe.

The sight of the clouds soothed my broken heart, gently drying the tears which had claimed me from the time I woke up to find Mom was gone, until I climbed my neighbor's steps. I was lost, but the clouds comforted me. Years later, I asked that neighbor if she remembered the clouds from that day. She didn't, but it didn't matter. I did. From time to time, those clouds visit my memory, and I smile. Because everything did in fact, turn out alright.

These days, in addition to being an outstanding wife and mother (my family's words, not mine), I'm also an outstanding licensed therapist. I love my family and I love my work. Both are fulfilling, which makes a compelling impact on those with whom I come into contact. To me, I am at the upper echelon of my profession, the world just hasn't met me yet.

My children are proof that I'm a great mother. With God and my husband's help, they are productive and thriving, breaking stereotypes and curses that plagued my family for generations. Teen pregnancy, single parenthood, low education – it all stopped with my kids. I'm not boasting, I'm bragging on God. And I'm not afraid to do so! I give Him all the glory for my successes, and credit myself for the work that I've done in accordance with His will for me.

Spiritually, I'm walking fully in my call. I'm a student again, working on a second master's degree, with a 4.0 GPA. I am connected to a next-level ministry and use my gifts to serve in various capacities, including the counseling center. I'm not a minister in my congregation; however, I have a thriving ministry. I'm committed to breaking stereotypes and misconceptions about faith and mental health.

My congregation is comprised of my clients who use their faith to cope with hardships. Our sanctuary is our Zoom meeting room, where members can log on as I virtually help strengthen their minds and heal festering wounds. My flock includes the ones God divinely places in my path because He knows I have something they need. So no, I am not a licensed minister yet…but my ministry is in full effect. Since I've already received God's approval and authority, I can wait on earthly endorsements until He orchestrates the appointed time for me to be ordained. It's going to come.

I've learned to wait.

I'm still in therapy, but for maintenance. When I accepted my call, a new set of issues surfaced, so my treatment shifted to developing my spiritual self and gaining the confidence to believe what God says regarding my destiny. I still don't know His ultimate plan for my life, and that's fine. I don't need to know. I have enough faith that He will never lead me astray. Though His directives are at times painful, the hurt is temporary. Just as the Psalmist David proclaims, *"Weeping may endure for a night, but joy comes in the morning."* (Psalms 30:5).

Therapy has taught me to address pain, process it, make responsible decisions to manage it, and wait for morning to break. Morning *always* breaks. I'm never stuck in the muck and mire of life's disappointments; the other side of frustration doesn't always look like what I expect and I've learned to accept that, too.

What surprises and delights me the most is the confidence I have in myself. I have a voice now, and I'm not afraid to use it to defend myself and others. I'm no longer waiting for Mom to fight my battles, which she'd do without hesitation. I'm strong enough to speak up for everyone who has yet to find their voice. I'm confident in my abilities and not afraid to be wrong. Errors are where learning occurs.

One of my greatest victories came during my first semester at Virginia Union University. I only listened in class because it was filled with established preachers. I (wrongfully) assumed they knew more than me. After all, they were giants and I was a grasshopper, too afraid to share my beliefs until a male student made some assumptions about black women that ticked me off. I politely let him have it! From the responses I received from the class, I learned my thoughts mattered.

Following that incident, I vowed never again to assume less of myself. I don't need to be a cookie cutter image of what a minister is supposed to be by society's standards; it's okay to be me, just as I am. My views tend to be different from some of my peers, my perspectives challenged by others, and I don't care. The only thing that matters is that I show up and present my authentic self, ready to learn, debate, and challenge not only others' perspectives but my own.

Seeing my faith grow and how I've managed to let go of those things that were hindering me (grief, people, and disappointment) brings a smile to my face. All those things I held close and valued over myself, I released so I can live. See, being alone is peaceful. Of course, that's because I hear my thoughts as well as those of my Creator with clarity allowing me to identify what makes me happy. Finally, I stopped forgoing my desires and interests for the wants of others. My needs matter most; I matter and I'm truly free to be me. I've taken center stage in my own life.

Grief no longer has a grip on me. May I share something with you? It's alright not be consumed by what we *think* we need. It's all about perception. Allowing ourselves to be swallowed by grief leads to further suffering. Now of course, there are usually other factors that contribute as well. For me it was low self-esteem, rejection, and resistance to God's plan. Grief was the catalyst for my dysfunction. Eventually, God pushed me to evaluate my life, my relationship with Him, and take responsibility for my healing. I had a choice: Wither in pain and continue blaming God, my mother, and myself for my sorrow, or get over it.

Despite God granting us free will, what would choosing to wallow in the spirit of defeat teach my children? They were watching every move I made—intensely focused on every decision. They'd be subject to my same mistakes instead of learning from them. My children's livelihood depended upon me making the right choices—Godly choices. I was better off with God, and smart enough to move out of His way.

I've learned that God removes people from our lives for His own reasons. They were never really ours to begin with; he loaned them to us for a season. When He takes them away, we feel sad, angry, and sometimes joy. No matter the reason, their removal is for our purpose, even when we don't fully understand.

Some people are removed because they'll cause devastation in our lives, or we'll destroy theirs. Some die because dying is better than what's ahead. Still, others are taken from us to make room for those meant to impact us, while others leave because we've made them our god.

In all of this, we offer God the least of us. People receive the worship, time, resources, and loyalty we should be extending to Him. That's what happened with Mom. I made her my god. Her presence was preventing me from moving into my destiny. I'm not arrogant enough to believe this is the only reason, but the reasons are irrelevant. Please understand God isn't just working in your life, He's working in the lives of everyone else at the same time. He's so powerful, He can orchestrate multiple destinies as He sees fit. He's not only concerned about you, but also His other 7.7 billion children in the world. He causes *all things* to work together for *the good* of those who love Him and are called according to His purpose (Romans 8:28).

God moves may not always make sense; however, they are necessary. The *good* isn't always what we desire. They can be downright painful, like the death of a loved one. And even though it doesn't feel good at first, eventually it turns out to be for our good. Our responsibility is to surrender to God and cherish the precious moments He's put in our care. Loss can't be avoided – we all experience it at some point in our lives. But when it hits us, we have to feel the pain, let go, and move forward.

We can't be afraid of getting close to someone God has directed into our lives because we're afraid of losing them. That's where my hesitation to build friendships comes from – I want to keep them forever. My challenge has been pushing past anxiety to allow the relationship to naturally develop into the season it's intended for. No matter how long their season lasts, I know I'll be blessed to have them in my life.

It's taken a lot for me to move forward to spiritually understand God's purpose for taking both of my moms from my life. The key was getting my mind and heart on one accord. Then, I completed a ritual of release. This ritual is based on our individual needs and may look different to all of us. For me it consisted of me visiting my mother's and mother-in-law's gravesites. Armed with flowers, my husband and daughters went with me, knowing I wouldn't be able to let go of two mothers alone.

That day, I knelt beside both my mothers' headstones cleaning off the dirt as my family remained by the car, supportive as they gave me my time alone with my favorite ladies. As I laid the fresh flowers in place, I began to speak. Told them all about life since they'd left me. Expressed my gratitude for their help in becoming the woman I am. Said how much I missed them, that all they invested in me was paying off. Finally, I thanked them for helping me reach this point in my life. I was alright. Better than alright, actually. I was happy and at peace and made sure they knew it. The tears flowed as I poured out my heart; peace settled deep in my spirit, and I let them go.

Do I still get sad? Yes. However, now I recognize where it's coming from, which makes it easier to regroup and figure out how to resolve it. For years, Christmas was hard. Where I used to decorate the house, wrap presents, and do everything I could to make the holiday special for my children, eventually I decided since no one wanted to help me take down the decorations, I stopped putting in the effort to continue this great tradition. The truth was that was an excuse. Residual grief caused me to be resentful, not my family. Mom died December 17th. Mama Lucy died December 15th. Two different years, same amount of pain.

December remained dark for years. Every holiday, I did my best to push through until the day after New Year's and all the holiday hoopla died down. Once again, therapy rescued me. Last year, I actually got excited about Christmas! I bought a tree with all the trimmings, gave gifts to people I didn't normally consider giving gifts to, played music, and truly enjoyed the season. It felt like Heaven! I was breathing again, genuinely loving life and everything in it. The chains of sadness were broken; I was free to just be.

Now what? Freedom is what comes after bondage. It's what we do after we lose everything. It's how we accept, acknowledge, and move forward. Sadness is inevitable. Seeking professional help, practicing self-care, or finding focus through a higher power helps us work through it when it comes. Accept whatever God is causing to manifest in your life, including freeing yourself from being bound to people, places, or faulty perceptions. Believe God. Not just *in* Him…believe Him. Believe what He says about you and surrender to His will. Don't be afraid and allow grief, depression, or low self-esteem to keep you from the destiny He's planned for you. Walk proudly in your purpose! Take your rightful place in the driver's seat, knowing the end that initially hurt was just the beginning of the best to come.

My favorite poet, Maya Angelou, once said, "*Every storm runs out of rain.*" No matter what life throws at us, there's comfort in knowing it won't last always. Not every storm is destructive; some of them are for security. Sounds strange, but it's true. The storm of losing my mother ultimately protected me from settling for mediocracy. There's so much in me that wouldn't have come to fruition had she lived. Simple things like buying my first home, getting married, graduating from college, and developing a true sense of self may not have flourished had she lived.

You may be thinking, *"Sure they could have."* Hear me out: I was so comfortable being Mom's shadow, depending on her was effortless. Besides, my siblings were doing the same thing, so why wouldn't I have followed in their footsteps? The storm required me to answer my call, discover my gifts and *use* them. The heartbreak and tragedy were necessary. Not just for me to know how they feel, but for me to effectively serve others. Before I could serve, I needed to develop and truly grasp the notion that I can handle anything with God's help. That's what storms do - develop and give us the confidence that we can make it through.

The Bible says in Psalm 23, *"Yea, though I walk through the valley of the shadow of death...."* Mom's favorite Psalm. At some point, we'll come out on the other side. Crises make us feel helpless; however, we're not meant to stay in the storm. At some point, the sun will shine again. Morning will come.

As for me, God rescued me from the weighted blanket of dysfunction I was so comfortable in, and ushered me into a life filled with love, happiness, and fulfillment. I've made it through. The sun has driven all the clouds away! I'm at peace, I'm free, and I'm transformed. The love of my life is gone...but I've landed securely in my *"now what?"*.

What's next for you?

About The Author

Mavis G. Rowe is a native of Portsmouth, VA. Her personal motto is "If you don't like something, change it. If you can't change it, change your attitude."-Maya Angelou. Mavis is a licensed clinical social worker who currently works with the geriatric community and has over twelve years experience in mental health. She holds a master's degree in social work from Norfolk State University and is pursuing a second master's in divinity at The Samuel Dewitt Proctor School of Theology at Virginia Union University. She's passionate about empowering women to excel beyond the social and political constraints that bind them. Mavis is a proud wife and mother of 6 adult children. She is a member of The Mount at Chesapeake where she volunteers with several ministries. She is also an Amazon Best Selling Author. Her first book, a collaboration with 11 women of faith, "Removing the Fear: A Truth Journey from Fear to Freedom" was released in March of 2022.

Contact Mavis at:
m.rowe.lcsw@gmail.com
To purchase her books, visit mavisrowe.com

www.ingramcontent.com/pod-product-compliance
Lightning Source LLC
Chambersburg PA
CBHW072012290426
44109CB00018B/2213